THROWN TO THE WOOLFS

THROWN TO THE WOOLFS

JOHN LEHMANN

HOLT, RINEHART AND WINSTON
NEW YORK

Library of Congress Cataloging in Publication Data
Lehmann, John, 1907–
Thrown to the Woolfs.
Includes index.
1. Lehmann, John, 1907–   —Biography.   2. Woolf,
Leonard Sidney, 1880–1969—Biography.   3. Woolf,
Virginia Stephen, 1882–1941—Biography.   4. Hogarth
Press.   5. Authors, English—20th century—Biography.
I. Title.
PR6023.E4Z519   1979   821'.9'12 [B]   79-1925
ISBN 0-03-052191-2

First American Edition—1979
Originally published in Great Britain

Printed in the United States of America
1 3 5 7 9 10 8 6 4 2

CONTENTS

ILLUSTRATIONS

INTRODUCTION

By 1931, when John Lehmann began working for Leonard and Virginia Woolf at the Hogarth Press, the dark basement offices at 52 Tavistock Square contained the most glamorous publishing enterprise in England, one of the most intriguing in the history of publishing.

It had begun unpretentiously, almost off handedly, in 1917, when Leonard conceived the idea of using the physical labor of printing as relaxation for Virginia, a kind of work therapy, forcing her mind to rest from its exhausting imaginative labors. For under £20, they bought some type and a small handpress, which they installed on the dining room table (they were then living at Hogarth House in Richmond), and, with the aid of a sixteen-page instructional booklet, they taught themselves to set the type, impose it, lock it up in chases, and print a decent page. Within a month they considered themselves proficient enough to attempt a little pamphlet consisting of Virginia's "The Mark on the Wall" and Leonard's "Three Jews," which they bound together and titled *Two Stories*. Printing one page at a time, they produced one hundred and fifty copies. They stitched the books themselves, using carefully chosen Japanese paper for the covers. They considered the venture such a success that their next, Katherine Mansfield's story, *Prelude*, was even more ambitious. At sixty-eight pages, it was twice as long as *Two Stories* and would have taxed their patience if printed one page at a time on their handpress, so they enlisted the cooperation of a local printer. Virginia set the type in borrowed chases that could hold the type for four pages, and Leonard carried them to the cooperative printer's large treadle platen press on which he ran them himself.

The Woolfs' original aim was to print poetry and short works of prose that commercial publishers would not be interested in. They intended to do all the printing themselves, and, accordingly, in the third year of the Hogarth Press, they printed and bound T. S. Eliot's *Poems* and Virginia's *Kew Gardens*. But *Kew Gardens* was given a favorable notice in the *Times Literary Supplement*, and they received so many orders for it that they had to subcontract the production of a second edition to a commercial printer. With that step the Woolfs began transforming themselves from hobbyist printers into publishers, and although they continued to print and bind some books themselves—including *The Waste Land* in 1923—more and more works were printed for them. Unintentionally, even somewhat reluctantly, they had started a viable business.

The history of the Hogarth Press is exciting because it suggests the triumph of imagination over capital, the creative mind over the managerial. Since the Press was a hobby, since they had other sources of income, the Woolfs did not have to make a profit from it. So they enjoyed the tremendous luxury of publishing only books they thought were good. And because they knew so many of the finest writers and thinkers in England, interesting books came their way. Little more than a year after the establishment of the Hogarth Press (if one can describe so grandly the setting up of a handpress on a dining room table), they were offered the manuscript of *Ulysses*, and it is a sign of the Woolfs' literary acumen that they agreed to publish it, although much about the book shocked and displeased them. Sadly, a printer willing to risk prosecution by setting such "obscene" material could not be found, and the manuscript had to be returned to Harriet Weaver, who had offered it to them. But other exciting manuscripts followed. S. S. Koteliansky, who was passed on to the Woolfs via Katherine Mansfield, wanted to bring out in English Gorky's *Reminiscences of Tolstoi*, recently published in Moscow. Koteliansky and Leonard Woolf translated the book, and Hogarth published it in 1920. Not only was it a great success, but it also marked the beginning of a fruitful collaboration and of the Hogarth Press's distinguished list in Russian literature. In 1922 alone the Woolfs published Bunin's *Gentleman from San Francisco*, Dostoevsky's *Stavrogin's Confession*, and *The Autobiog-*

raphy of Countess Tolstoi. Another prestigious and profitable coup was Freud's collected papers and the International Psycho-Analytical Library, which came to them through James Strachey, Lytton's brother and an early disciple of Freud. But the Press's greatest asset would prove to be Virginia herself. Her first two novels had been published by her half brother, Gerald Duckworth, but printing "The Mark on the Wall" and *Kew Gardens* herself must have given her a taste of what must surely be a fantasy for any writer—being one's own publisher, subject to no control, no judgment but one's own, with the great power of producing and distributing oneself what one has written. The connection may be no more than accidental, but it is certainly true that her first completely distinctive and original works were the first works that she and Leonard published themselves, the collection of short stories called *Monday or Tuesday* (1921) and *Jacob's Room* (1922).

In undertaking to produce Virginia's works, they realized they were making a commitment to becoming serious publishers, and so, for the first time, they hired someone to help them. Ralph Partridge, the first in what was to be a long and distinguished series of assistants and managers at the Hogarth Press, came to them in 1920, on a part-time basis, and by 1923 they were able to publish thirteen titles, some of which they printed and bound themselves, some of which they only printed, some of which they had printed commercially. Even the books printed for them bore a personal touch, for the Woolfs supervised the design themselves, still searching for interesting papers for the covers or hiring innovative artists to create jackets. Vanessa Bell, for example, designed the jacket for *Jacob's Room*. Inside and outside, Hogarth Press books defied conventional expectations and were recognizably the products of distinctive personal tastes. But the inside, the content, always took precedence, distinguishing the Hogarth Press from so many other small presses that took as their model the Kelmscott Press's devotion to finely printed books in fine bindings, an ideal the intellectuals of the Hogarth Press considered precious.

As Virginia Woolf's reputation as a novelist grew, the Hogarth

Press prospered. After 1925 and the publication of *Mrs. Dalloway*, she became more than a coterie writer. *To the Lighthouse* sold well, *Orlando* even better. Vita Sackville-West, whose work they had started to publish in 1924, proved to be a popular author too.

Ten years after its foundation, the Hogarth Press had become a successful commercial venture and an important institution in the literary life of London. True to its unconventional beginnings, the Press continued to implement new ideas: the Hogarth Essays, the Hogarth Living Poets, the Hogarth Lectures on Literature were all series that gave the public good writing it could have obtained in no other way. By 1930, six years after moving to Tavistock Square and establishing the Press in the basement, the Woolfs employed three women as bookkeepers and typists and a professional salesperson. They were handling twenty to thirty titles per year. Anyone who has seen the skyscraper offices of New York publishing firms will appreciate the singular achievement, be it comic or miraculous, of a firm that carried out all aspects of publishing except printing—that is, editorial work, publicity, orders, and shipping—in the basement of a London townhouse. And remember, too, that the heads of this firm were working at it only part-time—Virginia, for one, carrying on a career as novelist and essayist that would have been exhausting for many stronger people.

Determined to keep their own work at the Press part-time, but determined, too, to run an efficient and professional organization for the sake of their authors, the Woolfs realized they must hire a full-time manager. The first was George Rylands, a young Cambridge graduate who left to accept a fellowship at Cambridge. He was followed by Angus Davidson, who in turn was succeeded by the sixteen-year-old Richard Kennedy. None of these men found it easy to get along with Leonard Woolf, who demanded much of them and paid very little. John Lehmann was the next to arrive. Virginia described him at the time as "a tight aquiline boy, pink, with the adorable curls of youth; yes, but persistent, sharp." He was twenty-three, a graduate of Eton and Cambridge, a poet. There is a middle-class fatality, a bias toward abstraction, that turns young men who want to be construction workers into architects, prize-fighters into trial lawyers, printers into publishers. Lehmann, like the Woolfs, began by wanting to do some printing; the only printing he would ever do at the Hogarth Press was of stationery and labels. But printing's loss was publishing's gain, for Lehmann proved to be a talented, sensitive, and innovative editor, an inspired literary entrepreneur. In 1932 he produced *New Signatures*, a book famous in its time, which, by putting together such poets as Auden, Spender, C. Day Lewis, Empson, Eberhart, Julian Bell, and Lehmann himself and by presenting them as a united front, created in the minds of the public a new literary movement. Again, through *New Writing*, a twice-yearly anthology, Lehmann was instrumental in bringing to public attention the politically committed, generally leftist work of young writers in the late thirties. Perhaps his greatest achievement was *Penguin New Writing*, published periodically in a cheap format, which served throughout World War II to introduce new poets and prose writers to a public hungry for descriptions of its own experience. In his eight years with the Hogarth Press and his seven years in his own firm, John Lehmann, Ltd., he was one of the most exciting figures in English publishing.

For the Woolfs Lehmann was invaluable, bringing them into contact with the talented young men of another generation. He brought them Spender as a friend, Isherwood as an author. Virginia was almost fifty when he first came to work for them. Lehmann could articulate for her the viewpoint of the younger generation, arguing the importance of political commitment as Europe moved toward war. They hardly ever agreed, but the argument helped to keep her from ossifying mentally, when success and age might well have induced a hardening. I don't think Lehmann himself appreciates his importance to Virginia Woolf at this time. She had surprisingly few people close to her whose literary taste she respected, with whom she could discuss her own writing, and several of her most interesting letters about her own work were written to her young colleague at the Hogarth Press. It was Lehmann who stimulated her to write "A Letter to a Young Poet," one of her most significant—if irritatingly defensive—literary manifestos.

Lehmann was "thrown to the Woolfs" first in 1931 as manager of the Press, with the prospect of becoming a partner after two years. Julian Bell, Virginia's nephew, warned Lehmann that it would not be easy to get along with Leonard: that he had a bad temper, was interfering, overbearing, obstinate, argumentative, and eccentric in his business methods—all of which proved to be true. But the romance of the Hogarth Press was so strong that Lehmann, like the talented people who had preceded him, could not resist giving it a try. The Press seemed to him itself "a work of art," a business still small enough to represent a distinct statement of personal taste. And then there was Virginia. Lehmann's attitude toward her was one of reverence and awe, for her luminous beauty and magical presence almost as much as for her talent.

Lehmann's portrait of Leonard Woolf is usefully unworshipful. We have heard enough from others about Leonard the saint, but no man is a saint to his business associate. We see through Lehmann's eyes a man unnaturally repressed, a man so terrified of unruly emotion that he harnessed his life to overwork and a series of exacting, punctually executed routines, a man braced to handle major crises but thrown into hysterical rages by small disorders, a man tight with money, always certain he was right. He got Lehmann to do a great deal of work—to talk to authors, to write advertising copy, to keep track of reviews for usable quotations, to prepare sales leaflets, to help with the budget and inventory, even to travel the provinces taking orders. But he did not allow him any real power—that is, a voice in what was published. Lehmann could merely suggest; the Woolfs decided. As the time came for the promised partnership to materialize, Leonard became more and more difficult. He himself has admitted that he liked to run things, did not willingly share or delegate his power. The Hogarth Press seems to have reminded him of his youthful career as a colonial administrator and to have brought out the patriarchal strain in him.

When Lehmann left in 1932, he was not replaced, and by 1938

the Woolfs were again desperate for someone to take the burden of the Press from them, so desperate by now that they at last agreed to accept Lehmann as a partner. He bought out Virginia's share, although she continued to read and pass judgment on all literary manuscripts and to pitch in occasionally with the manual labor. For the next three years, except for members of the family, no one had a chance such as Lehmann for observing the Woolfs at close range. Thanks to him we can watch Virginia relating some incidents in the life of Flush, Elizabeth Barrett Browning's dog, the subject of Virginia's mock-biography. As she tells the stories, she laughs so hard that her face turns red, she cries, she cannot continue, and has finally to be led away by Leonard. We see her with Lehmann and Leonard Woolf at Monks House, relaxing after dinner in a room filled with books she has bound herself and with lilies, gloxinias, and begonias raised by Leonard. Leonard puffs at a pipe that keeps going out. Virginia smokes a cigarette she has rolled herself. And the conversation turns to sex, with the woman who was so curious about other people's passions asking most of the questions.

Later, Lehmann was privy to the despair that preceded her suicide, trying to restore to her the faith in her own work that she had so utterly and disastrously lost. As Lehmann continues the story of his association with the Hogarth Press after Virginia's death, it becomes clear what a difference she made in that enterprise. Whether or not she was formally a partner, her taste and imagination had been crucial in literary decisions. It is always gratifying to realize that rejections may mean a failure of imagination and competence on the part of the publisher and not of the writer, but there is a particular edge to one's enjoyment of Lehmann's accounts of being unable to persuade Leonard Woolf to publish Saul Bellow or Jean-Paul Sartre.

Thrown to the Woolfs provides fascinating glimpses of the Woolfs in their workaday life, but it does more than that: it is a uniquely valuable account of English literary life in the thirties and during the war years, and, particularly, of the Hogarth Press. The story ends with the dissolution of the partnership between Lehmann and

Leonard Woolf and the absorption of the Hogarth Press into Chatto & Windus. The Hogarth Press continued, but the romantic story of the political journalist and the great novelist whose hobby turned into an artistically and commercially successful institution was over. If psychoanalysis had been likely to have helped Virginia Woolf, one might have cause to regret her choice of therapy. As it is, it seems wholly fortunate that Virginia and Leonard Woolf had old-fashioned notions about salving mental unrest and, instead of spending hours talking to psychiatrists, decided to spend them in printing and, eventually, in helping to bring the works of other talented writers before the English-speaking public.

PHYLLIS ROSE

ACKNOWLEDGEMENTS

My warm and appreciative thanks are due to the following, who have permitted me to quote from letters which they wrote to me or in which they hold the copyright as literary executors: Professor Quentin Bell (Virginia Woolf, Vanessa Bell, Julian Bell); Mrs John Carleton (Michael Roberts); David Higham Associates (Louis MacNeice); Mr Roy Fuller; Mr Christopher Isherwood; Mrs Ian Parsons (Leonard Woolf); Mr George Rylands; Mr Stephen Spender; the Society of Authors for the Strachey Trust (Lytton Strachey); Mrs Henry Yorke (Henry Green).

My thanks are also due to my sister Rosamond for permission to quote from her essay which appeared in *Recollections of Virginia Woolf*; to the Hogarth Press for quotations from Leonard Woolf's autobiography; and to Sussex University Library, the New York Public Library (Henry W. and Albert A. Berg Collection), and the Humanities Research Center at Austin, Texas, in whose collections many of the letters quoted, from Leonard Woolf, Virginia Woolf and Julian Bell, are housed.

JOHN LEHMANN

FOREWORD

My connection with the Hogarth Press, which had begun in January 1931, came to an end, coldly and finally, at the beginning of 1946, when the partnership between Leonard Woolf and myself was dissolved. This partnership had lasted for nearly eight years – years which had seen the Munich crisis, the outbreak of war with Nazi Germany, the Blitzkreig on London, Virginia's death, and the final victory of the Allies in Europe. A troubled and stormy time; but a time I look back on as one of the most fruitful and stimulating in my life. The partnership was preceded by a period of nearly two years, which ended in September 1932, when I worked as a trainee Manager, and which forms the subject of the first part of this book.

In 1946 I was too busy laying plans for my future, as editor and publisher, to spend much time in bitter regrets or sorrowful reflections. The chance to put my recollections in order, to try and see the experience in some kind of perspective, did not come for another eight years, when I began to write my memoirs. Since the publication of *The Whispering Gallery* and *I Am My Brother*, however, a great many letters and other documents have come to light, dug from the dusty depths of my own files. Leonard's five-volume autobiography was published before his death in 1969, and much illuminating first-hand reminiscence has become available from, among other sources, the great work of Virginia's diaries. New thoughts, new insights, new material, have all made me feel that the tale can and should be retold, and that by doing this I may be able to make a much fuller contribution to the history and understanding of that remarkable creation of the Woolfs, the Hogarth Press, as well as fill in gaps in my own record. There is, after all, plenty of evidence that interest in the Press, and many misconceptions about it have been growing simultaneously in recent years, and on both sides of the Atlantic. The temptation to look again is all the greater because my three volumes of autobiography are long out of print, even in their abbreviated one-volume American edition, *In My Own Time*.

I have not confined myself to my relations and work with the Woolfs themselves, but have tried to give a picture of my relations with the writers who were already, or came to be, published by the Press while I was working there: as I look back, I see them in some ways as the most refreshing and creative part of the whole experience. And I have made as much use as possible of letters, both to and from myself, in order to give the life and atmosphere of the time as vividly as possible.

My thanks, alas posthumously, must go to my friend Cyril Connolly, for having suggested the title of this book, when we were looking through Leonard's letters only shortly before his death.

PART I

LEONARD AND VIRGINIA

I EXAMINED the little colophon again. It puzzled me. Was it a dog's head against the speckled background in that ring? An alsatian? A borzoi?

Then the penny dropped. Of course it was intended as a wolf's head. It appeared on the title page of a novel I had just read, *To the Lighthouse*. I had fallen instantly in love with it. Since that time – the year after it was published in 1927 – I have reread it at least a dozen times, and am still in love with it.

I had been urged to read it either by Julian Bell, who had only recently come up to Cambridge but had already become one of my close friends, or by George (Dadie) Rylands, young and brilliant lecturer in English literature at that time at King's (which was also Julian's college, while mine was Trinity). Or perhaps by both independently. It was the first work of Virginia's that had come my way, and I felt I had made an overwhelming discovery.

Dadie, who was a friend of my sister Rosamond, undertook the task, at my insistence, of being my guide among the modern writers. No guide could have been more patient, more teasingly encouraging, more stimulating. I was full of eager curiosity about the whole scene, having hardly got beyond A. E. Housman and Bernard Shaw while I was at Eton. There was, however, one, more modern, exception: Lytton Strachey. I had discovered his *Queen Victoria* and *Books and Characters* during my last two schoolboy years, and read them avidly, after lights-out, with a torch under my blankets. Rosamond, who had already achieved instant fame with her first novel, *Dusty Answer*, promised me an introduction to the great man himself. It seemed almost too good to be true.

Julian and I both wrote poetry, and though we were very far from being the only fledgling poets among our contemporaries at Cambridge, we found an affinity almost at once. This must have been, I think, because we both wrote nature poetry, for our ideas

about *how* to write were very different. I was deeply tainted with
romanticism, which Julian regarded with increasing suspicion as
his passion for the eighteenth century developed. We used to have
long discussions about every poet under the sun, poetic techniques,
schools of poetry, and the misdeeds of our Georgian elders –
though we did not always agree about who the chief culprits were.

During the next few years, as our friendship grew, these discussions were carried on with ever greater intensity. They were
continued by letter during the vacations, and in the frequent
visits we paid to one another's country homes. At Charleston, the
converted farmhouse in Sussex where the family lived, I came to
know Julian's mother, Vanessa. From the beginning she showed
me affection and sympathy, and very soon I was one of her most
devoted, loving admirers.

What I find curious now is that during these visits we never
went over to Monk's House at Rodmell, only a few miles away,
where Leonard and Virginia spent their weekends. That meeting
still had to wait until I had gone down from Trinity in 1930, and
took place in London.

Julian succeeded in having a first book of poems accepted (by
Chatto & Windus) before me: *Winter Movement* was published
in the autumn of 1930, much to my delight. I had already gone
down, and had been travelling about the Continent, trying to get
a slim volume into shape myself, rewriting lines and stanzas,
finishing poems that had still remained unfinished at Cambridge,
alternating between hope and confidence and the discouragement
of moments when the whole small achievement seemed worthless.
Nevertheless Julian's steady encouragement buoyed me up, and I
finally sent off a typescript for Dadie's inspection, as he had
generously promised to pronounce a verdict. I had complete
confidence in his judgement.

Not only was the verdict favourable, but he promised to show
them to the Woolfs for their series, the Hogarth Living Poets, in
which I had already appeared as a contributor to the anthologies

of *Cambridge Poetry* in 1929 and 1930. Dadie had worked with the Woolfs as Manager for a short period some years before, and had been rescued from that not altogether happy experience by winning his fellowship at King's. During that time he had helped the Woolfs in the actual printing of some of their booklets of poetry, and had found such pleasure in it that he had conceived the idea of buying a small press of his own. In the course of our long walks together he talked to me about this, and found that I, who had become deeply interested in William Morris and all his works while at Eton, also had a secret wish to do just the same. The result was that we began to plan to buy a press together: we even went to see a manufacturer to find out what it would cost us. When Dadie took my poems to Leonard and Virginia, he mentioned this to them. As it happened, they were in one of their frequently recurring states of looking for a new assistant and Manager.

A few days later the letter arrived that was completely to change my future. I had originally been intended by my parents for the Diplomatic Service, of which my first cousin Sir Ronald Campbell was already a distinguished member, and had spent vacations with French and German families to improve my languages. Then my godmother, Violet Hammersley, had heard of a vacancy in the Prints and Drawings Department of the British Museum and, knowing my fondness for the Old Masters, had put me in touch. This struck me as a just preferable life; without the many excitements that might have come my way as His Britannic Majesty's representative in foreign capitals it would, I thought, give me plenty of leisure for writing poetry. I started my education in the subject at once by making a prolonged visit to the famous Albertina collection in Vienna. This letter, however, altered everything in a flash. Leonard wrote, on 19 December:

We like your book of poems very much and would be glad to publish them. I propose to send them now to Lady Gerald who edits our Hogarth Lecture Series and see whether she agrees with us to do them in the autumn season. I am afraid that we are full up for this spring and that our spring list is already printing. I hope you will not think it too long to wait for the autumn.

Dadie, whom we saw yesterday, talked to me about your possibly wishing to come to the Press and become a publisher. We ourselves are in some doubt as to the future, for the Press is taking up much more of our time than we care to give it. I should like to have a talk with you on the subject. Would there be any chance of your being able to come and see us when we return after Christmas about January 6th?

Leonard made a slight slip-up in this letter. Lady Gerald (Wellesley), later to become the Duchess of Wellington and known in Bloomsbury as Dottie, was editor of the Living Poets series and not the Lectures. She was an all but passive editor, because as far as I could make out she never proposed a poet herself, though from time to time she would object to a poet the Woolfs wanted to publish, and sometimes be more enthusiastic about a manuscript they were very dubious about themselves. The important thing was that she subsidized the series. On this occasion she approved of my poems, and the way was therefore clear, without any awkward hitch, for me to join the Press if everything worked out right. I rushed off to see the Woolfs, in a state of high excitement, the moment they got back from Rodmell – a little later than they had told me. On 12 January 1931 I wrote to Julian:

I would have written to you before about the poems, if the end of last week had not been so hectic – interviews – consultations – calculations. I expect you know substantially what the offer of the Woolves was going to be: I was surprised when they made it to me – on Friday, at tea, when I met them both for the first time, and thought them most charming, Virginia v. beautiful – and not a little excited. I've now decided I'm going to make every effort to accept the offer, but must first see my Trustees, stockbrokers, etc., and discuss further details with Leonard. It may be a little difficult to find all the money, but I hope all will be well if L. doesn't suddenly put up the price! How I should like to see you to discuss it all, and hear your opinion. I really can't imagine any work that would interest me more, and to be a partner with them, with a voice in what's to be published (and how) and what isn't – it seems an almost unbelievable stroke of luck. . . .

Evidently the blood of my Scottish ancestor, Robert Chambers, who with his brother William had founded the publishing firm of W. & R. Chambers a century before, as well as *Chambers' Journal* and *Chambers' Cyclopaedia*, was stirring in my veins, and playing a rather more important part in my hopes and visions than dreams of William Morris and the Kelmscott Press. My mother was soon brought on to my side and, pleased to think I might be launched on a career so obviously closer to my aspirations than diplomacy or museum expertise, did her best to make the family trustees look on the opportunity with favour. Julian, however, while obviously pleased at the turn of events, rather distrusted my starry-eyed enthusiasm, and sent me a cautionary letter as soon as mine reached him:

What I wanted to talk about was the Woolves. I've had two long talks with the pair of them, and have had to give a complete character of you. They're extremely enthusiastic for the plan, and naturally I egged them on. The result is, I feel a certain grain of responsibility – anyway, I think it probably is my business to be officious and meddling. The point is, Leonard has had very little success as an employer – witness Dadie and Angus Davidson. I know that he's apt to lose his temper, and also to be rather interfering and overbearing, also obstinate and argumentative. I expect he's a good man of business, but rather eccentric in his methods. Besides this, as they probably told you, it's a job that involves an enormous amount of very hard drudgery – probably more even than the Museum would.

It seems only fair to tell you all this about Leonard, since I did as much about you to him. I don't know a great deal at first hand, but remember how Dadie hated the job, which by all accounts is distinctly a difficult and heavy one.

Perhaps I should also tell you that they said to me that if you could not take the partnership they would still try and get you to take the job as Manager at a salary. Only then of course you would have no decisive voice in the books published – I think you may anyhow find Leonard slightly dictatorial about that.

Well, there are the disadvantages as I know them. I hope they won't deter you – it would be superb to have you there, and I should feel much more hopeful about the future of English literature with you at the Press. It's a serious thing to 'sink your capital in such a concern' but I expect it would be more amusing than most jobs.

Julian's letter had been, I feel sure, a difficult letter to write, because of his divided loyalties: to me, as one of his closest male friends on the one side, and to his Aunt Virginia on the other. When I reread it today, I honour him for the concern and candour, so characteristic of him.

Intensive negotiations followed between Leonard, myself, and my family trustees. Leonard liked to work out very meticulous estimates, for all possible contingencies, about the duration of my probation, the various stages of salary during that probation, and the extent of my share in the business at the end of my apprenticeship, which was to last two years. Several schemes were suggested and discarded, either because my trustees, or Leonard himself, saw objections. He was at his most characteristic during these negotiations: he revelled in figures. Eventually an agreement was reached which satisfied all parties. I was in such a hurry to fix everything up that it seemed to have taken a long time, but in fact only six days after I had first given Julian the news I was able to write to him:

This week has been a fevered one – I emerge with an agreement in my pocket, by which I become Manager of the Hogarth Press in October – if not fired after eight months of apprenticeship. And I have the option of becoming a partner in a year or two. And I start on Wednesday as ever is! I'm much excited, and would like to talk it over with you soon. Your advice was just what I wanted – very welcome. As a matter of fact Leonard had lost confidence in his first proposition even before my Trustee turned a dubious eye on it, so I think both parties feel better under the present agreement that we argued out in a series of interviews. I pray that I shall be a success: hard work, but congenial – and the power of helping in a publishing business that is still small enough and intellectual enough to be a work of art – and

Leonard is giving me good holidays, long enough to get some writing done, I hope. But there's so much I want to say, that I can't say it all in a letter, and must wait till I see you. I was charmed by both Leonard and Virginia, and hope they liked me. . . .

The news travelled very fast among my friends. Michael Redgrave, who had been one of the editors of the undergraduate magazine, *The Venture*, with which I had been associated at Cambridge, and was still hesitating between a literary and a stage career, wrote: 'I am overjoyed at your news, and please accept my loving congratulations! This is the beginning of great things.' Dadie, whom I had not been able to consult during the rush of negotiations, wrote that he wished he could have a talk with me about it, and told me to step warily and drive a bargain. At the same time Lytton Strachey, whose attitude towards his old friend Leonard was always a little ambivalent, was writing to Roger Senhouse:

The latest scandal is that the Woolves (aided and abetted by Dadie, of all people) are trying to lure John Lehmann to join the Hogarth Press, and put all his capital as well as to devote his working hours to doing up parcels in the basement. And the large ape is seriously tempted.

Lytton was of course thinking of the unfortunate experience of his secretary and beloved friend, Ralph Partridge, who had worked for the Press as Manager in the early days. Needless to say, I did not know of this letter at the time, but, in his private conversations with me, Lytton had hinted teasingly at possible rocks ahead. In any case, no one could say that I had not been warned.

At that time the Hogarth Press occupied the basement of No. 52 Tavistock Square, Bloomsbury, to which address it had moved when the Woolfs left its birthplace, Hogarth House in Richmond, in 1924. As it has vanished now, I had better describe it. It was one of the terrace houses built in the great development of the

Duke of Bedford's London estate at the turn of the last century.
James Burton and his successor, Thomas Cubitt, could be described
in modern terms as speculative builders; but what they built was
simple and durable and modestly elegant, though without the
distinction of Bedford Square which belongs to a slightly earlier
period. Thomas Cubitt completed the south side of Tavistock
Square, in which No. 52 lay, after the end of the Napoleonic
Wars; the front looked north towards the Euston Road, and its
back windows south towards the British Museum. The ground
floor and first floor were occupied by a small firm of solicitors,
who held a sub-lease from Leonard. Above them were the living
quarters of the Woolfs: the sitting room, dining room, bedrooms
and Leonard's study. The walls of these rooms were attractively
decorated with murals by Vanessa Bell and Duncan Grant.

The Press was housed in the semi-basement. In the front room,
obviously once a kitchen, with an original old-fashioned dresser,
lay the main administrative office where the typists had their
desks. Behind was a smallish windowless room, where parcels of
Hogarth books likely to be in immediate demand were kept.
Down the corridor, on the right, was the former scullery, which
the Woolfs had turned into their printing room. In my time the
first treadle machine dominated it, with stacks of type beside it
against the wall. There was also a ramshackle lavatory, in which
old Hogarth galley proofs were provided as toilet paper. Beyond
that was a small room with capacious cupboards built against one
wall, which may have been a housekeeper's or butler's room in
the old days. This was my room, as Manager. It had a window
looking out on to an outside corridor, which led to the big studio
room at the back. This latter, I conjectured, had been built on at
some time during the nineteenth century, over what had been a
small garden or paved space. It was used as an additional stock
room, but also, more importantly, as a work room for Virginia.
She had a large stripped wooden desk in it, surrounded by the
piles of parcels of Hogarth books straight from the binders, which
also overflowed into the corridor.

In his slyly entertaining book, *A Boy at the Hogarth Press*, Richard Kennedy, the youngest of my predecessors, does not identify the Manager's room at the back, but it can be seen in his map as an empty space at the end of the corridor. The whole semi-basement gave the impression of dilapidation and draughts. My room was badly in need of redecoration. It was warmed by a small ancient gas fire, which gave off very little heat, and in front of which Leonard on his regular morning visits would try to warm his hands, without any marked success. The window was dirty, and nearly always stuck. On one occasion, in the spring, in need of fresh air, I tried to open it, but I only succeeded in breaking one of the panes and covering my hands with blood.

None of these disadvantages discouraged me in my first year. I was on sacred ground, an initiate in a temple whose grubbiness he hardly noticed. And all around me were not only the untouched binder's packets, but also opened packets containing the remaining copies of books that were already precious to me, such as Virginia's *To the Lighthouse* in its original light blue binding, and her *Monday or Tuesday*, the little book that announced the beginning of her new style, horribly printed on atrocious paper but with Vanessa's original linocut illustrations; Ivan Bunin's short story masterpiece, *The Gentleman from San Francisco*, E. M. Forster's *Pharos and Pharillon*, and *The Notebooks of Anton Chekhov*, translated by Leonard in collaboration with Koteliansky, in its mottled paper-over-boards binding. I searched in vain for those two most famous of the first half dozen productions of the Hogarth Press, T. S. Eliot's *Poems* or Katherine Mansfield's *The Prelude*; but I persuaded Leonard to let me have, for my own library, copies, where they still existed, of the early volumes of poetry that he and Virginia had printed themselves, all different shapes and sizes and many of them in the prettily designed paper covers which they had bought from Roger Fry's Omega Workshop. My collection eventually included John Crowe Ransom's *Grace After Meat*, Herbert Read's *Mutations of the Phoenix*, Robert Graves's *Mockbeggar Hall*; and little books almost entirely for-

gotten today, some I think unjustly, such as Fredegond Shove's
Daybreak, Hope Mirrlees's *Paris*, Nancy Cunard's *Parallax*, and
Dadie Ryland's *Russet and Taffeta*. I longed to take a hand in the
printing of more books like these myself, but the odd thing is that,
though the Woolfs were at work on one or two little volumes
while I was there, and though my interest in printing had been
one of the reasons that had brought me to the Press, I never did
more than roll off some labels and sheets of writing paper. I was
far too busy with my work as Manager.

The routine was regular on five days of the week. I would
arrive between 9 and 9.15 am from the rooms I had taken in
Heathcote Street just behind Mecklenburgh Square, a ten-
minute walk through the picturesque disused burial ground of
St George-The-Martyr. Leonard had a passion for exact punctuality, and may well have been watching my arrival from an upper
window, stop-watch in hand; but as I am by nature a punctual
person I was more likely to be at the Press a few minutes early
rather than a few seconds late. There is a story told about one of
my predecessors, that according to Leonard's time-piece he had
arrived two minutes late one morning. He denied it, pointing to
his own wristwatch which indicated precise punctuality. They
argued hotly for some time, until Leonard called a taxi and drove
with the hapless young man to check by Big Ben. A rare occasion
on which Leonard's conviction that he always knew best got the
better of his parsimony.

Shortly after my arrival he would come down, the day's correspondence in his hand, discuss it with me and give me instructions for dealing with it. He was at his best during these sessions in
the first few months of my apprenticeship: kind, patient, and
often extremely amusing. I think he particularly liked to have a
neophyte sitting at his feet, absorbing his wisdom; it was later,
when the neophyte began to have ideas of his own, that trouble
could start. He had his own pungent views on the book world
and the publishing trade. He had, after all, taught himself to be a
publisher the hard way, and had also had long experience, as a

literary editor as well as author, of the foibles, fantasies and prejudices of other authors, reviewers and booksellers. His comments could be caustic, devastating; he was particularly funny about the representatives of the various printers and paper-makers who came to see us. I think these homilies were a very good education for me into the mysteries of the career I had chosen. Even if his descriptions sometimes made me feel that I had walked into a Looking Glass world far stranger than Alice's, he managed to inject my idealism with a necessary drop or two of cynicism without destroying it. Leonard himself was, in general, cool and philosophical about the ups and downs of publishing; his fault was in allowing trifles to upset him unduly. A penny, a halfpenny that couldn't be accounted for in the petty cash at the end of the day would drive him into a frenzy that often approached hysteria, while invoices, purchases and payments on the spot were checked and re-checked by a crushed staff that was obliged to stay late and made to feel miserably guilty. He had a congenital tremor, which had saved him from military service in the war, and on these occasions his hands shook like aspen leaves in a gale. On the other hand, if a major setback occurred – a new impression, say, of a book that was selling fast lost at sea on its way from the printers in Edinburgh – he could display a sage-like calm, and shrug his shoulders.

Leonard's conviction that he could organize everything better than anyone else, so strongly in evidence during his colonial years, was shaken by these petty upsets in a way that was quite grotesque (to use a word he was very fond of himself). It is, I now think, surprising that there was not a more rapid turnover of staff in view of these recurring persecutions and the all too modest wages the young assistants were conscious of being paid; but they were in a way bewitched by the aura of the Press and the enchantress-like presence of Virginia in the background.

One of the advantages of the Press was that, being a small and very personal concern, there was no nonsense of rigid compartments. Everyone was expected to do everything, particularly the

Manager. In those early months I was thrown in at the deep end, and had to deal with authors who came to see us (except Leonard's special political cronies), write to them about their manuscripts, comb the reviews for useful 'quotes', design advertisements to exact specifications, prepare sales leaflets, make up estimates, and keep an eye on the stocks of books that were enjoying a steady demand. All this I found fun, though hard work: what I did not enjoy so much was travelling the provincial booksellers with advance copies and information about forthcoming books. This is really a seasoned expert's job, but Leonard was extremely reluctant, for reasons mainly of economy, to employ professional travellers. He sent me out almost as soon as I started work on a round of the main bookshops in the Midlands, the North, and Scotland. My reasons for liking the books were not by any means always the reasons that appealed to hard-headed booksellers when ordering copies from a small publishing house known for its highbrow and specialist, rather than popular, appeal. Some busy buyers were brusque, withering, almost rude. 'No, I don't think we can sell any of that title. . . . None of our customers are likely to be interested in this. . . . I suppose Mr Woolf has a good reason for publishing that series. . . . Well, we'll order one copy of the new novel by this unknown chap, and three on sale or return. Can't promise to move them. Book trade's in a very bad way' (it always was). 'Too many books are being published' (there always have been). 'I hope you'll have something by Mrs Woolf or Miss Sackville-West next time you come round.' I stood there nervous, tongue-tied, my promotion talk sticking in my throat. Sometimes, however, I found myself sitting in a small office beside a bookseller who really cared, who tried to put me at my ease, and enquired genially how Mr and Mrs Woolf were. Such booksellers might even be persuaded to order two copies of a new volume in the Hogarth Living Poets – my own, for instance. I went out assuaged, with a list of orders in my hand that would probably pay for my night in the hotel, and relieved to have some positive news to send in my daily letter to Leonard.

I wrote to Julian at the beginning of March:

I wonder what you've been reading lately. I've confined myself almost to Hogarth books, partly new books that had to be read before I set forth, MSS to be criticized, and old books of our authors, such as Plomer and Kitchin. Fascinating, but a trifle submerging. But I think that in the summer I can begin to think of poetry again. Leonard and Virginia are being generous with holidays, and I don't mean to let my Muse, fragile invalid though she is, be smothered by fiction.

Travelling the provinces was a curious experience, utterly depressing when they were sulky and crabbed all the books, exhilarating when they were friendly and were (or appeared to be) influenced by one's persuasions. Edinburgh was looking very beautiful, and it was amusing to meet Harry's relic of the '90s – André Raffalovitch. I also saw something of Peg [my sister Beatrix who was playing in Scotland at the time], and took Elsa Lanchester to an odd cinema one evening while the play was on (she was up with Charles for a few days, and v. bored with Scotland and the Scotch, out and out cockney that she is), so there were plenty of friends. . . .

One of the books that smoothed my path a little, because it had been published soon after my arrival, and was already having a distinct success, was *Saturday Night at the Greyhound*, a first novel, sent to the Press in the previous autumn, by John Hampson Simpson (who called himself John Hampson), a young man who lived in the Midlands where he had the job of looking after the retarded brother-in-law of a rich businessman. I had written to Julian in the middle of February:

Hampson seems to me a great hope. (I was disappointed to find that his wildly obscene homosexual stories have been returned to him. Virginia shouldn't have stimulated my curiosity.) Oddly enough, the book is already going very fast, embarrassingly fast when the first edition is quite small. We've already ordered a second. I trace it to a puff by Harold Nicolson, good friend to the Press that he is. . . . A swarm of new ideas hovers round 52 Tavistock Square. It really is absorbing and exciting at the moment. I wonder, on the other hand,

what the Woolves think of me! Perhaps they've already hinted my
imminent dismissal to you, this week-end. . . .

The fact that they decided to go on a car trip together a month
or two later, and leave the running of the Press to me indicates
clearly, I think, that they were happy with their new Manager.
Virginia seemed to put herself out to be especially friendly and
interested – in a young man who worshipped her with burning
devotion. She had written a description of me in her diary after
our first meeting: 'A tight aquiline boy, pink, with the adorable
curls of youth; yes, but persistent, sharp.' It was certainly necessary
to be persistent and sharp in running the Hogarth Press, with
Leonard's eagle eye upon me all the time, but as far as she was
concerned, humility before my conviction that she was one of
the great writers of our time, and wonder at her beauty, were my
dominant emotions. Edith Sitwell has written: 'Virginia Woolf
had a moonlit transparent beauty. She was exquisitely carved,
with large thoughtful eyes that held no foreshadowing of that
tragic end which was a grief to everyone who had ever known
her.' I think my sister Rosamond's description most exactly
coincides with my own recollections: 'She was extremely
beautiful, with an austere intellectual beauty of bone and outline,
with large melancholy eyes under carved lids, and the nose and
lips, the long narrow cheek of a Gothic madonna. Her voice,
light, musical, with a throaty note in it, was one of her great
charms. She was tall and thin, and her hands were exquisite.'
I have written elsewhere of the occasions when the Woolfs
invited me up to their part of the house, for lunch followed by a
working session, or to join an after-dinner party where I would
meet many of the Bloomsbury luminaries. But every day I would
see her, soon after Leonard's early visit, passing across my window
on her way to the studio, to spend a morning at her work; and
once she paced to and fro outside in the narrow passage, reading
the manuscript of Julian's poems which he had just sent in. I think
this was done for my benefit, so that I could tell Julian that his

work was receiving what is called in publishers' jargon 'prompt consideration'. Virginia read and gave her opinion on all the literary manuscripts offered to the Press, though I don't think she bothered about the purely political or socio-political manuscripts which she considered entirely Leonard's province. I would also sometimes find her in the scullery-printing room setting up type, which she continued to enjoy doing as a relaxation from her creative labours; though many of the letters were apt to be put into the frames upside-down, and had to be corrected by Leonard. When a book boomed and orders were heavy, she would often join Miss Belsher, Miss Strachan and Miss Walton in the front office, doing up parcels. Young authors, coming in to leave a precious manuscript and dreaming of encountering the famous author, would never suspect that they were actually in her presence as the figure in the drab overalls busied herself with scissors and string.

One of the 'swarm of new ideas' I had mentioned to Julian was a kind of anthology of contemporary Cambridge verse and prose, a 'symposium of work being done by the younger generation at Cambridge', as we described it. In the middle of March I wrote to Julian, who was staying in the village of Elsworth with his girl-friend Helen:

I broached the subject to Leonard today, and found him remarkably sympathetic. He said however that we should have to get out some more definite plan for him to see, before he could give or withhold his benediction. I think he agreed with me that it must be both critical and creative. I was very excited that he seemed to think well of the idea, as ever since we talked it over it has been becoming more attractive to me, I see such possibilities in it.

At any rate he is going to let me take charge of the idea, and if we mean to make anything of it we must get going at once. Leonard rightly says that it would be just the sort of book that might sell well as a Christmas book (provided we don't let it get too heavy), and therefore the sooner the compiling can start the better. We must discuss it when we meet on Friday. And I hope we may get a day or two in somewhere during the vac. to examine the question thoroughly.

Work was started at once, and we asked Dadie Rylands to act as our organizer in Cambridge. I can remember very little about it, except that it was to be political as well as literary, that William Empson was to be a star among the poets and Malcolm Lowry among the prose-writers, and Goldsworthy Lowes Dickinson to be asked to contribute a foreword. Things seemed to go wrong with it from the beginning – perhaps the idea was too vague, or the mixture wouldn't work – and by the end of July it had been abandoned. If it was to appear as a Christmas book, the contributions would have had to be in our hands within a few weeks; Dadie had despaired of mustering them in time, and 'Goldie' had decided against writing the foreword. We talked hopefully of carrying it over to the spring, but by then another idea had overtaken it.

In the middle of September I received a letter from a young man I didn't know, but who was aware that I was working at the Hogarth Press. His name was Michael Roberts, and he wrote:

I wonder if you would care to take a glass of beer or a cup of coffee one evening with a person who has, at various times, read your poems with pleasure – I expect Empson could have introduced us had he still been here, but in any case, even if you don't feel inclined to call, I hope you'll not be bothered by this note from a stranger. I'm at home most evenings.

This letter was, of course, far too flattering for me to ignore, and we did arrange to meet very soon after. Out of our meeting emerged the project of *New Signatures*. My first impression of the tall young man in glasses who opened the door of his flat to me, was of a giraffe that had taken to the serious life of learning, perhaps a university don of a giraffe. His gaze was sharp, rather formidable; but the rare, contracted smile that played across the strange zoo face was decidedly sympathetic, and soon we were talking about poetry and our contemporaries who wrote it as if

we had known one another for a long time. He had very decided
ideas; and one of them was that the Cambridge poets who were
to have contributed to the Miscellany – Julian, Bill Empson,
Richard Eberhart – all had much more in common than had
appeared to us in the midst of the dramatic confrontations that
Julian had insisted on. What was more, he saw an affinity between
us and the new young poets from Oxford who had just emerged
over the horizon, W. H. Auden and Stephen Spender, and two
poets who had already been published by the Press, Cecil Day
Lewis and William Plomer. I was carried away by the persuasive
enthusiasm of his arguments: we all represented a reaction
against the poetry that had hitherto been fashionable, not merely
the already damned Georgians but T. S. Eliot as well, and those
who were trying to follow in the footsteps of the French
Surrealists. We were far more modern, he asserted, we were
united by a desire to assimilate the imagery of contemporary
life, even when writing about nature (as Julian and I did), we had
totally discarded the sentimental clichés of our predecessors; we
were all looking for a new intellectual and imaginative synthesis,
which would be positive and not pessimistic in its attitude to the
problem of living in the twentieth century. Neither in my mind,
nor in his, was there any suggestion as yet of the radical politics
which within a year or two were to be so closely associated with
what, largely through *New Signatures*, came to be known as the
'Pylon' school of poets, and which could be heard in the poems
which Stephen Spender eventually contributed. What was
needed, he finally claimed, was an anthology to rub his arguments
in and make the sluggish public sit up and take notice.

Not entirely convinced I was nevertheless fired by the idea,
and felt pretty certain that in his preface he would make his case
as skilfully and persuasively as he obviously knew how. I got him
to agree to include A. S. J. Tessimond, a young poet of striking
originality with whom I had come into contact in London. I
talked it all over with Leonard the next day, and found him
surprisingly sympathetic. Michael Roberts was given a contract

almost at once. *New Signatures* came out the following spring, and made even more of a mark than we had hoped. The reviewers were impressed, a second printing was soon ordered, and there was a general feeling in the air that something had happened in poetry; even though Cecil Day Lewis was already known as a poet and Wystan Auden had published his first book of *Poems* in 1930. Michael Roberts was never completely satisfied with his Preface, and holes have been picked in it often enough since then; nevertheless it worked. In the not entirely rational world of literary judgements it was taken to 'mark the beginning, the formal opening of the poetic movement of the 1930s'.*

William Plomer was one of the new acquaintances I made in London through the Press, and it was not long before we became close friends, a relationship which lasted until his death. We published his novel of Japan, *Sado*, during that first spring, and I found something in it that deeply attracted me, though I do not now think it is one of his best works – perhaps spoilt by a little too much moralizing. The opportunity to get in touch with him soon came, as among my first jobs was the preparation of publicity for *Sado*. When I wrote to him asking for some details of his life for the blurb, he replied:

> Please say I am English, *not* South African. My age is 28. My career, though chequered so far, has not been without its oases – or is that a mixed metaphor? I went to school at Rugby, I haven't attended a university, and don't intend to do so. I have been a trader in Zululand and an apprentice farmer in the (rugged) mountains on the Basutoland border. I have been unemployed in Japan, a tourist in Russia, and an alleged Λορδος in Greece. I once saved a nun from drowning. I seldom eat tripe, etc., etc. What *am* I to say? ... If you mention that I have written verse, please say I never pretended to be a poet – even to myself.

What struck me at once about the fairly solid-looking figure, of rather more than medium height, with the deep voice, who came into my office in the basement one morning, was the sharp

* *Journey to the Frontier* by Peter Stansky and William Abrahams.

but twinkling look behind the magnifying spectacles, the sensitive poet's mouth, and the humorous animation that would suffuse his features at the slightest lead from whoever he was talking to. As I got to know him more intimately, I found his delight in anything eccentric or fantastic, the continuous bubble of crazy commentary he would keep up among responsive friends, completely irresistible. I noticed, too, that in some quite mysterious way, when one was in his company, preposterous things would happen, outlandish freaks would appear, that were exactly the right food for his peculiar brand of nonsensical foolery. Like so many imaginative people of lively personality he seemed to create his own surroundings. He would pounce on items of news, or elicit stories from his intimates that were precisely on his own wavelength; as, for instance, when he wrote in a letter to me about this time that he had just met a man 'who tells me that there is now a regulation in the Roumanian army that no one below the rank of Major may use lipstick'.

Leonard urged me to read his first novel *Turbott Wolfe*, written in Africa when he was only twenty-one. He sent it to the Woolfs in 1925 without much hope that they would publish it, but they accepted it at once and published it as soon as a printers' strike allowed them. What struck me about it was the passion with which it was written, the ferocity of its rejection of all prejudices and conventions that stand in the way of justice and the natural flowering of human feeling. But what impressed me even more deeply was 'Ula Masondo', an utterly original prose poem that I found in his next book, the collection of short stories called *I Speak of Africa*. It is the story of a simple Zulu boy who goes to work in the gold mines, is nearly killed in an underground fall of rock, and is finally so corrupted by his new surroundings, the civilization of the white man, that when he returns to his home village he rejects his family and his native upbringing. 'Ula Masondo' is told with sustained, electrifying imaginative power; but what moved me particularly was the capacity he revealed to enter into the minds of people living by patterns of impulse and belief completely other than those of modern Western society. It is a quality that I have found and treasured in all his stories whether of Africa or Japan or even of Greece. And in his London stories, too, this uncanny gift of empathy is shown in his portraits of unsophisticated people who find themselves in a society that is alien and often bewildering to them. William had also, at the time I first knew him, already written a good deal of poetry, but, as he himself knew, had not yet found his authentic voice as a poet.

William and I had a long and happy relationship, not only as friends but as author and publisher. I had not, however, introduced him to the Press, as I was to introduce Christopher Isherwood.

Just before I started working for the Woolfs, my sister Rosamond brought Stephen Spender over one day to lunch at our family home at Bourne End. He was twenty-one, but already beginning to create a stir in Oxford with his earliest poetry. In the afternoon we went for a long walk together by the Thames, up river towards Marlow. Very tall and slim, with a huge head of untidy curls, he loped along beside me in the mild winter landscape, pouring out his views on the world, on how to find fulfilment and how to write, and graphically described the life he had adopted in Germany, where he spent most of his time. He talked a great deal about Auden, who shared (and indeed had inspired) many of his views, and about their mutual friend, a certain young novelist called Christopher Isherwood, who had settled in Berlin in stark poverty and was an even greater rebel against the England we lived in than he was. It was clear that he and Auden revered him as a great writer of the future. He told me that Isherwood had been deeply disappointed at the way his first novel *All the Conspirators* had been received, and that he had failed so far to find a publisher for his second novel, *The Memorial*.

Stephen, a great maker of legends, liked to see his most intimate friends and fellow-writers in a dramatic light: they were a closeknit, almost heroic band, the creators of a new literature. I think he felt he had not adequately put me in the picture during that walk, and not long after he wrote to me from Berlin:

There are four or so friends who work together, although they are not all known to each other. They are W. H. Auden, Christopher Isherwood, Edward Upward and I. I only know Christopher and Wystan Auden of the other three, but I believe that Edward Upward, whom I do not know, has had a great influence on Christopher. Auden travelled to Germany, and that is how Christopher and then I came here. Whatever one of us does in writing or travelling or taking jobs, it is a kind of exploration which may be followed up by the other two or three.

Here was a manifesto to whet the appetite of any young poet who had taken up publishing, and I urged Stephen to get his friend to send me the typescript of *The Memorial*. When it arrived – in the early spring, because Christopher's agents were still trying other publishers after Jonathan Cape's refusal – I read it with mounting enthusiasm. Without too much difficulty I persuaded Leonard and Virginia to accept it, though they were a little hesitant at first and insisted on reading *All the Conspirators* before they yielded. 'I don't like it,' Leonard wrote to me, 'but it is distinctly clever.' We brought it out the following year, in an unconventional and highly original brown-paper jacket designed by John Banting. Though it had a comparatively small sale, it alerted several influential critics and literary pundits to its author's name.

Naturally I was very keen to keep in touch with him and his plans for future work. We did not meet until August 1932, in the Hogarth office on one of his brief visits to England, but the first surviving letter I have from him came from his Berlin address in the Nollendorfstrasse. It is dated 13 January 1932:

Dear Lehmann, Stephen tells me that you want me to write and let you know what I mean to do in the near future. At present I'm writing an autobiographical book, not a novel, about my education – preparatory school, public school and University. After this is finished I shall start a book about Berlin, which will probably be a novel written in diary form and semi-political. Then I have another autobiographical book in mind. And possibly a travel book. So you see, I have no lack of raw material! It is only a question of time and energy. . . . I am very glad that my novel is coming out so soon. I hope you will have more success with it than it deserves.

It seems clear that the 'autobiographical book' must have been the first draft of *Lions and Shadows*, which was not in fact published until 1938, overtaken by the Berlin stories which are mentioned immediately after. I must have written to urge him to give them priority, because in his next letter, dated 6 February, he writes: 'I'm sure you're perfectly right about the Berlin book. Unfortunately, however, I don't feel nearly ready to write it yet. I should probably have to get away from Berlin first. Whereas the other book is all in my head already.' He adds at the end of the letter: 'Has Auden sent you a long play called The Fronny?' This appears to refer to an unpublished play, though the title might suggest that it was a very early version of *The Dog Beneath the Skin*, which was not performed or published until 1935, an immediately previous draft of which, called 'The Chase', the two of them collaborated on early in the same year. In any case, Auden did not send it to me, and I do not seem to have tried to extract if from him, eager though I was to become the publisher of all the friends Stephen had mentioned. It should have been a chance for me to seize, as Christopher told me in his next letter but one (after the publication of *The Memorial*) that Faber & Faber, who had published Auden's *Poems*, did not appear to want it.

In the same letter, he writes:

Yes, I hope to let you have my novel in the autumn. If, that is to say, I don't scrap it. I'm afraid it's rather difficult to send you bits of it, as it is written entirely in the form of a diary, without any break in the narrative. It will have lots of characters and be full of 'news' about Berlin. I think the climax will be during these elections. Frank journalism, in fact.

Evidently he had changed his mind and had begun to work on *The Lost*, that 'huge episodic novel about pre-Hitler Berlin' as he called it later on. I think he was much encouraged by some good reviews of *The Memorial* (and enthusiastic letters he received) in spite of the lamentably small sales. From the island of Rügen on the Baltic coast he wrote to me in July: 'Please don't suppose that I'm disappointed by the sales of *The Memorial*. They are actually £1 more than I reckoned!! As long as one or two good critics like my work I am really quite satisfied. I am only sorry that I haven't been a financial success because I know that the Hogarth Press has lost money on me.'

After the first meeting our relations became gradually closer, though it was not until I stayed in Berlin in January 1933 that they grew really intimate. In *The Whispering Gallery* I wrote:

It was impossible not to be drawn to him. I was attracted by the warmth of his nature, and by the quality which appealed to me so much in *The Memorial*, an exact feeling for the deeper moods of our generation with its delayed war-shock and conviction of the futility of the old pattern of social life and convention; his capacity – the pressure he was under in his imagination –to invent the most extravagant dream situations of comedy for everyone he knew, evoked a response at once in that part of me that had produced the dotty fantasy plays at Eton; and at the same time I had fallen under the spell of his Berlin legend.

With a vivid recollection of that first meeting, I also spoke of 'the sense of alarm that seemed to hang in the air when his smile was switched off, a suspicion he seemed to radiate that one might after all be in league with the "enemy", a phrase which covered everything he had, with a pure hatred, cut himself off from in English life.'

In *Christopher and His Kind* Christopher comments amusingly on this:

John's intuition was correct. Christopher *was* suspicious and on his guard against this tall handsome young personage with his pale narrow quizzing eyes. . . . Seated behind his desk, John seemed the incarnation of authority, benevolent authority, but authority none the less. What Christopher didn't, couldn't have realized until they knew each other better was that this personage contained two beings whose deepest interests were in conflict; an editor and a poet.

The guard was soon dropped after this; and Christopher and I became, in a sense, close fellow-conspirators on the literary scene.

For the Hogarth Press the great event of 1931 was the publication of *The Waves*. Virginia had begun it (calling it *The Moths*) in September 1929; and it was on the completion of the *second* version, on 7 February 1931, that she had written in her diary: 'I wrote the words O Death fifteen minutes ago, having reeled across the last pages with some moments of such intensity and intoxication that I seemed only to stumble after my own voice, or almost, after some sort of speaker (as when I was mad). I was almost afraid, remembering the voices that used to fly ahead.' After that came the correction of this second version, but before she started on that work she and Leonard made their April tour of France, the highlight of which was the visit to Montaigne's tower at Brantôme. This tour gave her a much needed rest; but in spite of Leonard's judgement that the new book was 'a masterpiece', the correction of the typescript, and then of the proofs proved a severe strain. On 15 August she wrote in her diary: 'I am in rather a flutter – proofreading. I can only read a few pages at a time. So it was when I wrote it and Heaven knows what virtue it has, this ecstatic book.' The next day she added, 'I must stop after half an hour and let my mind spread, after these moments of concentration.' The headaches were beginning again, and Leonard had to tell her to take the proofs easily, and to rest as much as possible. I can remember seeing her during this time passing across the window of my office with a deeply careworn look; she was hardly able to answer when one spoke to her; she seemed withdrawn behind a veil, or like a somnambulist. When she had finally sent the proofs back to the printers, Leonard tells us that the headaches became even more severe, and he ordered her to stay in bed.

Vanessa's jackets have come to be thought of as an integral part of Virginia's books, the perfect sisterly accord of writer and artist sharing the same vision. In fact the truth was rather different.

Virginia asked me to send her a 'dummy' as soon as the printers had finally estimated the number of pages and we had chosen the thickness of paper. Vanessa wrote back to me from Charleston:

Thank you so much for the dummy. I will do my best to let you have a design soon. Until it is done I don't think I can decide about a coloured top but I will let you know then – I've not read a word of the book – I only have had the vaguest description of it and of what she wants me to do from Virginia – but that has always been the case with the jackets I have done for her.

The moment that was always the most agonizing for Virginia – the moment when her brain-child was exposed to the critical gaze of the public – was approaching. *The Waves* was published on 8 October. The advance copies arrived a few weeks before, and I seized one to read. I had just spent a weekend at Rodmell, and in my bread-and-butter letter I told her I was embarking on her book. She wrote back at once:

Lord! To think you are reading *The Waves*! Now I shall be interested to have your opinion – brutally and frankly – so please write it down for me. At present it seems to me a complete failure. And please don't tell anyone you've read it, because I'm already pestered with demands for copies, Hugh Walpole apparently having said that it's out.

By the way, are you nervous about your book? What do you feel about critics? I meant to ask you about all that; but was swept away by the tide of life at Rodmell. We enjoyed having you enormously, though in such a tempest of kittens and photographs. Some of them (the photographs) are good: not your portrait though. I'll send them.

All too typically, she noted in her diary: 'John L. is about to write to say he thinks it bad.' But John L. did not think so at all, and wrote to her with excitement and enthusiasm. So a few days later she was able to record in her diary that I, unlike Hugh Walpole who couldn't make head or tail of it, 'loved it, truly loved it, and was deeply impressed and amazed'. At the same time she wrote me a long, revealing letter, in which she described what effects she was aiming at in her new style:

It was, I think, a difficult attempt – I wanted to eliminate all detail; all fact, and analysis; and myself; and yet not be frigid and rhetorical; and not monotonous (which I am) and to keep the swiftness of prose and yet strike one or two sparks, and not with poetical, but pure-bred prose, and keep the elements of character; and yet that there should be many characters and only one; and also an infinity, a background behind – well, I admit I was biting off too much.

She added that she was afraid that in printing seven thousand copies the Press had absurdly over-estimated the demand. In this forecast she was very wide of the mark. In the first few months *The Waves* sold over ten thousand in the British market, and as many in the USA. I wrote to Julian ten days after it came out:

My hand [which I had cut badly] isn't so stiff now, and I've had the stitch out, so I can wield the pen, though not very legibly, I'm afraid, as I've had to start hot fomentations which means pompous and cumbrous bandages. All very unfortunate with your Aunt's book booming and high pressure of work in the office, the public apparently having decided that to be IT one must have *The Waves* on the drawing-room table. What did you think of it? – I don't believe you've said anything yet. . . . I was tremendously stimulated artistically by it – I wanted to go off and start experimenting in all sorts of ways at once.

Letters of praise and congratulation poured in, and Virginia's mood changed to a glow of happiness and pride. But even in the darkest months of doubt and anxious anticipation she had found some relief, as so often, in planning a new book. This was one of her 'holiday' books, *Flush*; originally conceived as a Christmas booklet, but soon developing into a full-length, serio-comic biography. I remember that I was in charge of the front office one day, when she came in, followed by Leonard, and told me she'd had the idea of writing a book about Elizabeth Barrett Browning's famous dog, Flush. They wanted to have it illustrated with photographs of their own spaniel, Pinker, in a variety of appropriate poses. She began to describe some of the episodes she'd already discovered. Leonard stood watching her and chuckling in the background. She soon became so carried away and almost hysterical with laughter, that she was red in the face and tears were streaming down her cheeks before Leonard led her off, incapable of going on.

I had already left the Press when *Flush* came out in the summer of 1933; but I was still there for the publication of her *Letter to a Young Poet* in July 1932. The Hogarth Letters series was one of the 'swarm of new ideas' that the three of us planned so eagerly in the first few weeks of my apprenticeship: little booklets in paper covers of six or seven thousand words in length, on all the topics of the day, and some – like our very first, E. M. Forster's *Letter to Madan Blanchard* – timeless. We roped in Raymond Mortimer to write on the French Exhibition at Burlington House that was one of the great artistic landmarks of the year; Leonard Strong to pay a tribute to W. B. Yeats; Viscount Cecil to write a *Letter to an M.P. on Disarmament*; and many other authors, Hugh Walpole and my sister Rosamond among them. We enjoyed ourselves planning them; they were not expensive to produce, and aroused much lively discussion. Virginia's contribution arose out of a plea I had made to her when I wrote so enthusiastically about *The Waves*. At the end of her (already quoted) letter in reply, she had written:

I think your idea of a Letter most brilliant – 'To a Young Poet' – because I'm seething with immature and ill-considered and wild and annoying ideas about prose and poetry. So lend me your name – (and let me sketch a character of you by way of frontispiece) – and then I'll pour forth all I can think of about you young and we old, and novels – how damned they are – and poetry, how dead. But I must take a look into the subject, and you must reply, 'To an Old Novelist' – I must read Auden, whom I've not read, and Spender (his novel I swear I will tackle tonight). The whole subject is crying out for letters – flocks, volleys of them from every side. Why not get Spender and Auden and Day Lewis to join in?

The idea lapsed for a while in the hurly-burly of the publication of *The Waves*, but revived when I sent her a copy of my book of poems, *A Garden Revisited*, which was published soon after. Revealing that she had by then changed her mind about the 'deadness' of contemporary poetry, she wrote:

I am a wretch not to have thanked you for your book, which will not only stand on my shelf as you suggest but lie beneath the scrutiny of my aged eyes [she was hardly more than fifty at the time]. I want to read it with some attention, and also Auden and Day Lewis – I don't suppose there's anything for me to say about modern poetry, but I daresay I shall plunge, at your bidding. We must talk about it. I don't know what your difficulties are. Why should poetry be dead? etc.,etc. But I won't run on, because then I shall spurt out my wild theories, and I've not had a moment to read for days – everybody in the whole world has been here. . . .

When *A Letter to a Young Poet* came out, in spite of the many passages of excellent advice, it caused a certain amount of dismay, even indignation among the young poets themselves. It was critical of our work, though she expressed her criticism with good-humoured urbanity but we thought with a rather surprising lack of understanding and fairness. Stephen wrote me a long letter about it, particularly irritated (not unnaturally) by her suggestion that we wanted to publish too young and ought to wait until we were thirty – all very well for a novelist, but where would the poetry of Keats and Shelley have been if they had followed that rule? She quoted (without giving names) from poems by Wystan, Stephen, Cecil and myself, and claimed, first, that we were too introverted, too interested in our own limited experiences, and, second, failed in our attempt to assimilate the raw facts of life into our poetry. Above all she claimed that we indulged too much in the sport of 'dressing up' and ranging ourselves into opposing schools and movements – a habit that was much more common, traditionally, in French than in English literature.

The whole tenor of her argument seemed to me to be at variance with her own bold striking out for revolutionary experiments a dozen years before. I wrote to her on the publication of the *Letter*, and maintained that if she had looked further she would have found poems to prove that we were far from being as self-absorbed as she claimed, and also that there was no harm in the 'dressing up' she attacked, that it was a good stimulant and in any case no new feature of the literary scene. She replied at length:

Of course dressing up may have some advantages; but not more than gin and bitters or evening dress or any other stimulant. Besides it becomes a habit, and freezes the elderly, like Wyndham Lewis, into ridiculous posing and posturing. But it's not a matter of great importance. I admit your next point – that is, that my quotations aren't good illustration; but, as usual, I couldn't find the ones I wanted, when I was working; and was too lazy to look. Anyhow, my impression is that I could convince you by quotations: I do feel that the young poet is rather crudely jerked between realism and beauty, to put it roughly. What it seems to me is that he doesn't . . . dig himself in deep enough; wakes up in the middle; his imagination goes off the boil; he doesn't reach the unconscious, automatic state – hence the spasmodic, jerky, self-conscious effect of his realistic language. But I may be transferring to him some of the ill-effects of my own struggles, the other way round – with poetry in prose. Tom Eliot I think succeeds; but then he is much more violent; and I think by being violent, limits himself so that he only attacks a minute province of the imagination; whereas you younger and happier spirits should, partly owing to him, have a greater range and be able to devise a less steep and precipitous technique. But this is mere guesswork of course. . . . The fact is I'm not at all satisfied with the Letter, and would like to tear up or entirely re-write. It is a bad form for criticism, because it seems to invite archness and playfulness, and when one has done being playful the time's up and there's no room for more. . . .

By that time Leonard and Virginia had obviously come to the conclusion that they could leave the running of the Press to me without worrying, and in the spring, before the Letter was published, set off for another holiday abroad, this time for a month in Greece with Roger and Margery Fry. I was perfectly happy about this, even though the trusty Miss Belsher who was in charge of the front office was absent much of the time, as I enjoyed my work, particularly when there was no interference from Leonard.

No one could have guessed from the letter Virginia sent me from Athens that the sun did not always shine on our relations:

I have written to you several times (in imagination) a full account of our travels, with a masterly description of Byzantine and Greek art (Roger is all for Byzantine) but I'm afraid you never got it. The truth is it's almost impossible to put pen to paper. . . . I'm afraid you've had the devil of a time, with Belsher away, and the doors standing open to bores of every feather. I've often thought of you with sympathy when one wheel of the car has been trembling over a precipice 2,000 feet deep, and vultures wheeling round our heads as if settling which to begin on. This refers to the road into the Peloponnessus. Then we went to Delphi, to Nauplia, to Mycenae – it's all in the letter I never wrote. I can assure you Greece is more beautiful than 20 dozen Cambridges all in May Week. It blazes with heat too, and there are no bugs, no inconveniences – the peasants are far nicer than the company we keep in London – it's true we can't understand a word they say. In short I'm setting on foot a plan to remove the Hogarth Press to Crete. Roger is the greatest fun – as mild as milk, but if you've ever seen milk that is also quicksilver you'll know what I mean. He disposes of whole museums with one brush of his tail. He plays chess when the dust is sweeping the pawns from the board. He writes articles with one hand, and carries on violent arguments with the other. It has been far the best holiday we've had for years, and I feel deeply grateful to you, for sitting in your dog-hole so stalwartly meanwhile. Excuse scribble. Love from us both.

The Woolfs returned to England in the middle of May. I started my own holiday soon after. When I got back, some crucial discussions took place between Leonard and myself. My holiday had made me rather restless. I felt that I wanted to be abroad more, and have more time for writing – or rather for what I imagined to myself as the complete poetic life; but the chief trouble was that Leonard was beginning to get badly on my nerves. I remembered all too clearly the warnings I had been given before I agreed to join the Press. I was beginning to learn what some of my predecessors had surely learned before me, that the truth was that both the Woolfs, but in particular Leonard, had an emotional attitude towards the Press; as if it were the child their marriage had never produced. As the time approached when it would be my right to enter into partnership – which Leonard with half his mind desired and needed – suspicion and tension between us grew, and reached at moments breaking point. I find in my diary, towards the end of June, the following note:

Leonard very difficult today, haggard, abrupt, twirling bits of string, a touch of hysteria in his voice, in fact suffering from a severe nervous crisis, cause unknown. This manifests itself in repeated invasions of the office, anxious examinations of work being done, nagging tirades and unnecessary alarms and impatience about what is progressing steadily and in advance of the time-table.

I did not want to leave the Press, but I was fed up with being a dog's-body, and I had begun to feel that Leonard and I could not go on any longer as we had been going for eighteen months. Leonard realized this – I put it to him as frankly as I could – and we began to discuss various alternative plans. At the same time difficulties had arisen in the office itself. Miss Belsher had fallen ill, Leonard was in great doubt about her future health, and began to look around for someone to take her place. On 5 June he had written me a very even-tempered letter:

We were glad to get your cards. I think, however, you misunderstand my attitude. There is, of course, no question of my desiring certainty or any kind of guarantee of permanence. How could that be possible? But we have the experience of 18 months behind us and it is from that that I feel that the *possibility* is that – not necessarily through any fault on either side – a similar situation will develop again. If I get someone else, I shall not have any greater certainty, but on the other hand I shall not start with a feeling of probable failure. However I do not think it possible to settle this by long range epistolary discussion and I propose to wait for a final discussion and decision when you return. The present position is that the negotiations with Miss Matheson have broken down. . . . I have therefore taken on a Miss Scott Johnston in Miss B's place temporarily until July 4th, but – frankly – at the back of my mind with the idea that possibly, if you and I decide to part, I might continue with her as a kind of Secretary Manager.

Dottie has turned against publishing anything in the autumn and thinks badly of MacNeice. She has returned the poems to me. I have read them again with less pleasure. I rather doubt whether it would be worth publishing them ourselves. What do you think?

This last paragraph was a severe disappointment, and added to my feeling of discouragement about the Press. I still wanted it to be the publishing centre for the works of the new generation of my contemporaries. Cecil Day Lewis we already had; Christopher Isherwood we had just succeeded in netting; Auden seemed irrevocably committed to Faber & Faber, and Stephen too, though I thought it possible that we might get his prose and therefore – eventually – his poetry as well. Louis MacNeice was not, strictly speaking, one of the group, and had not appeared in *New Signatures*; but the others admired his work as I did, and it would have strengthened my position immensely to become his publisher. He had written to me at the beginning of May:

Anthony Blunt suggests to me that I should send you some poems for the Hogarth Press. This (I hope you don't mind) I am now about to do. I happen to have ready a series of forty-odd poems arranged in progressive groups, but have no idea whether you would like them. Some of them are rather feeble individually but have their purpose in a series. I am therefore sending you about a dozen specimens.

The only thing is that some time ago I sent the whole series to T. S. Eliot, hoping Faber & Faber might do them. However, there have been so many hitches (i.e. Eliot losing everything and being generally inaccessible) that I am prepared to write to him and ask for them back. Which I will do if and as soon as you let me know that the Hogarth would do them.

I read the poems and was impressed by them, and wrote and told him I had put them forward to Leonard and Virginia with a strong recommendation. He replied on 10 June:

I am very glad you like some of my poems and shall be extremely pleased if the Hogarth decide to publish them. There are one or two (of those which I have not yet sent) which I am rather doubtful about, and whose inclusion I should like to leave to someone else's judgement.

Eliot, by the way, has suggested putting one or two of these same poems in the Criterion; I imagine the Hogarth Press would not object to this provided the Criterion published them first?

In spite of Dorothy Wellesley's unwillingness to publish Louis's poems in the Hogarth Living Poets series, I still had hopes of persuading the Woolfs to take them on at their own risk. Louis therefore sent me a typescript of the whole volume as he envisaged it, together with 'a tentative introduction or explanatory note'. I failed to change Leonard's adverse view, except to allow me to tell Louis that if they were resubmitted later in the year – i.e. when Dottie might be willing to subsidize further volumes for the spring of 1933 – there was a chance of acceptance. Louis obviously wanted the Press to be his publisher, and wrote again in July:

Many thanks for your letter and my MSS. I do not suppose I shall be doing anything with these poems in the immediate future so if the Hogarth Press would really like to see them again towards the end of the year, I should be quite prepared to return them to you.

I believe Anthony Blunt mentioned to you that I am doing a long essay on Humour in Latin literature which I hoped might possibly do for the Hogarth Lecture Series (if that is still going on). I think this should be quite interesting (at any rate for a work on the classics) and might even, if published, be bought by some of the lesser professionals at schools, etc. I don't expect to finish it till next year.

Nothing came of all this after I left the Press, and Louis MacNeice eventually joined the brilliant list of Faber poets.

Meanwhile Leonard and I had started the 'final discussions' which he had mentioned in his letter. We eventually came to a tentative new arrangement, though I don't think either of us was wholeheartedly enthusiastic. It seems rather, in retrospect, a desperate attempt to hold on to something that had already almost slipped from our grasp. He wrote to me on 24 June:

As agreed with you as a result of our conversations, I propose to put in writing the following terms of our new arrangement:

Our present agreement will terminate on August 31, 1932. From September 1, 1932, it is understood that you will not do more than two hours work daily actually at the Press. If you do not do the two hours work on any day, you will be prepared when the occasion arises to do more than two hours per day proportionately, this term being interpreted in a reasonable and broad way. During the period when advertising is being done, you will come on Thursday afternoons and supervise the preparation of the advertisements. Your duties will be managerial, general supervision, book production, and sales. In addition to your work at the Press itself, you will read the MSS for the purpose of preliminary sifting out and you will endeavour to get promising authors for the Press. It is agreed that if I am away from London at any time for not more than five weeks consecutively, you will exercise a general supervision over the Press and, when necessary, come for more than two hours, provided that your average daily attendance during the year does not exceed two hours. Your holidays will be six weeks in the year. You will receive as remuneration ten per cent of the profits and from September 1, 1932, to September 30, 1933, I will pay you monthly £16 13s 4d as an advance on this ten per cent, but it is agreed that the amounts paid shall not be returnable by you if the advance is not earned by the profits. The question of any guarantee or advance after September 30, 1933, is left completely open and it is understood that I do not pledge myself to any guarantee or advance after that date.

The present agreement shall be terminable at three months' notice, by either side.

In many ways this proposed new agreement was attractive to a young man who wanted to devote as much time as possible to writing poetry. Many young writers would have given their ears for it – always provided that they could have lived on £200 a year, even at 1932 prices. Of course much more might have come my way, if the annual profits of the Press greatly exceeded £2,000. But this seemed to me, at that difficult time, a dangerous hazard. Worse still, the new agreement said nothing about the partnership that had been promised me after two years salaried work as Manager.

All that summer I debated it with myself. The pull from Christopher and Stephen to start a new life abroad was strong; though it is only fair to say that in spite of their disinterested concern for my future as a writer – perhaps as a human being – they made it clear that they would be disappointed from their own points of view if I gave up my key position as *the* publisher in tune with their ideals. 'Come over to us!' they seemed to be saying, 'but don't be surprised if we're a bit sad.'

I confided my troubled doubts to Vanessa as well as to Julian, as my letter to him in the middle of July reveals:

I have teemed not only with bacilli recently, but also with schemes for the Hogarth Press. Now I'm afraid none of them will come to anything. Your respected Uncle wasn't exactly enthusiastic about any of them. And perhaps he was right. But all the same, with the material, the opportunities one has – I'd like to talk it all over with you some time. Have you been writing at all lately, outside your work? I haven't done a stroke – up to a week or two ago my mind was so occupied with negotiations with L. and V. that I became quite incapable of concentrating on anything else. And now I feel almost ashamed to have been so occupied with my own affairs so exclusively so long. Vanessa was a wonderful woe-receiver: I worship her. I'm afraid she got into hot water in the end – a little seems to have spilled on to a great many people. All my fault – I ought quietly to have left for Tahiti, no fuss, no sterile recriminations. . . .

In the end, and at the last moment, I made up my mind to go, on the date the old agreement expired. It was no doubt rather cowardly of me to leave without warning, but I felt that absolutely no profit could come from the renewal of long-drawn-out acrimonious arguments that had already exhausted me. And I had failed to convince myself that my relations with Leonard would ever, even under the new plan, recover completely from the abysmal state they were in.

Though he was, as I have shown, well aware that a break might come, Leonard chose to be outraged by the manner of my going, and hadn't a good word to say about me for a long time. Virginia – if one is to trust her diary, though one must remember that Leonard always had the right to read it – followed suit. I was distressed to think that in getting free of Leonard I had broken my ties with her too; otherwise I felt nothing but relief, and my friends were full of sympathetic understanding.

PART II

INTERLUDE: MAINLY
IN CENTRAL EUROPE

I HAD made up my mind to go somewhere abroad, where I could study and make myself intimately acquainted with the unrest that was boiling up in Europe beyond the Rhine; not to Berlin where Christopher was, at least not at first, but, I finally decided, to Vienna, to which I had always been drawn for reasons not absolutely clear to myself. I wanted to be alone and think hard, by myself, about all the problems that were running through my mind.

Above all I wanted to devote as much of my time as possible to writing poetry, and developing a new vein which I had already begun to explore in London before I left. Several of these new poems had been published by the sympathetic and perceptive young literary editor of the *Listener*, Janet Adam Smith, and her enthusiasm, as well as the warm approval of several other friends to whom I had shown them, encouraged me to persevere on these new lines. I was haunted by the passage in Rilke's *Notebook of Malte Laurids Brigge*, which was my constant companion:

In order to write a single verse, one must see many cities, and men and things; one must get to know animals and the flight of birds, and the gestures that the small flowers make when they open out in the morning. One must be able to return in thought to roads in unknown regions, to unexpected encounters, and to partings that had long been foreseen; to days of childhood that are still indistinct ... and to mornings by the sea, to the sea itself, to oceans, to nights of travel that rushed along loftily and flew with all the stars. . . .

Rilke had been one of my favourite poets, one of my chief inspirations since I had discovered his work in the Hogarth Press. His poems, and the sublime, almost fortuitous lyrics that break out of the prose visions in Rimbaud's *A Season in Hell*, marching cries in a dreaming wanderer's life, and the delphic utterances of Yeats's 'Crazy Jane' poems that seemed to me to have something of the wild spontaneity of songs that come out, unforced and pure, as if the will had nothing to do with them, thoughts transformed by the creative imagination into the simplest utterances; these were my ideals, the lights by which I wanted my new poetry to be guided; perhaps into prose forms as well as verse, discovering natural rhythms.

At the same time another process was taking place in my mind. Like many others of my generation I wanted to break out of the bounds of my middle-class life, to look for new sources of strength in the lives of working-class people who had never been subjected to the discipline of middle-class assumption and education. It was partly a scarcely conscious impulse of empathy, partly a mood created by our steadily increasing awareness of political issues as the world slump developed and the tragedies of impoverished unemployment stared us ever more starkly in the face; followed rapidly by the radicalization of our political views as what seemed to us the failure of social-democratic, reformist remedies spread from the disastrous General Election in Britain in 1931 to more and more of Europe; while the Soviet Union put out the cleverest propaganda to persuade us that the revolutionary, communist way was the only way that would solve the crisis. In my diary at the time – the autumn of 1932 – I tried to explain the problem as I saw it:

This is then my dilemma: and I suppose the dilemma of hundreds of others like me. On the one hand I see the moribund state of the culture I have been brought up in. The need to reject its shams and pretences if I am not to become a complete cynic. The need to be transplanted to fresh ground. On the other hand I have been educated in and accustomed to the old culture, my habits and states have been formed by it. My roots are fairly firmly embedded in the exhausted ground. Go and live among the workers, take part in their activities, make friends with them, work with them if you can, refuse to have anything to do with the bourgeois world, says one voice. And another: but practically all your friends belong to that world, you cannot break all the old ties. And what's more, you're totally unfitted to think as they think and work as they work; you lack the background and training of circumstances.

So we stand between two worlds, uneasily contriving makeshift compromises to placate conscience and reason.

Of course, as I very soon came to realize, I could not 'go and live among the workers', particularly among the Viennese, whose rooted idea of an 'English gentleman' was someone like Mr Brownlow in *Oliver Twist*; but I determined to acquaint myself with the plight of the unemployed in Austria, and those sections of the Viennese population on whom the slump, particularly acute in Vienna, bore most heavily. This, then, was the main subject of the poems I was writing during that first autumn in Vienna, Inevitably, however, I was gradually drawn by my explorations into the political cross-currents of the time, and became aware of the threat to the social-democratic government of the capital, which had built the magnificent new workers' housing estates, from the anti-democratic movements which drew their strength essentially from the countryside. This threat seemed remote enough that autumn; but things were moving very fast in Germany across the border, and the star of Hitler was rising. I went to stay with Christopher in Berlin in January, and witnessed the collapse of the Weimar Republic and the outbreak of the Nazi terror. The rest of 1933 was a time of uneasy and increasing tension in Austria, of the slow retreat by the Social-Democrats in the face of increasing arrogance and provocation by the other side; culminating in the desperate and disastrous insurrection of February 1934, which completed the rout of the anti-fascist left. For the next four years the Austrian government, Catholic and authoritarian, had to perform an agonizingly shaky balancing act between the (at that time) opposing power postures of Mussolini and Hitler; with the strange, and to me engrossingly fascinating situation that the Nazis were banished into illegality with the Socialists and Communists. Each maintained its own underground, and in addition there were secret splinter groups of all three. The events of 1933 and 1934 had, as I have already pointed out, driven me and many of my contemporaries further left, and while keeping in as best I could (as a foreign journalist) with all these underground movements, my greatest sympathy turned more and more towards the Communists.

My life in Central Europe became so absorbing for me, that my former life in London and my former circle of friends seemed to be receding ever more rapidly. I felt (as I have tried to explain in *The Whispering Gallery*) as if I were 'looking through the observation car at the end of a train that was gathering speed, making familiar landmarks diminish and bringing mountains into view beyond them on the horizon, mountains I had not known before existed'. I particularly minded this in the case of Julian, who had been so close to me for so long, and with whom I had shared the great passion of those earlier years – the first love of poetry. I am sure that Julian sensed this, for he wrote me a letter that touched me deeply in December 1934:

. . . All your old Cambridge friends are asking after you and hoping to see you. When we met we didn't find much chance to talk about poetry, because I feel that it's probably our best subject of agreement now. It's very hard for me to share your feelings about politics because we live in such different worlds. . . . But I've always felt that there's a certain intimacy between us as poets that should be able to last through any other difficulties of communication. Incidentally, do remember this difference in our lives when you feel that I'm unsympathetic. None of my friends are in danger or hardship, and it's hard for me to imagine what I should feel if they were.

Julian of course knew that I had gone a good deal further left in politics than he had at that time; but it is perhaps worth stating that he implied in this letter no criticism of my sexual life in Austria. He himself was unalterably heterosexual in his tastes; but he had known quite well of my affairs with my own sex before I left London, and was too civilized a Bloomsburian to take any attitude other than to hope that I was happy – and not taking too many risks.

My poems, both verse and prose, from that time reflected

increasingly my new revolutionary sympathies, and my horrified reaction to the terror in Germany and (in its much milder form) in Austria. Already by the early summer of 1934 I thought that I had assembled enough to make another volume, which I called *The Noise of History*. I sent them, as I was in any case bound by contract to do, to Leonard and Virginia, and received a friendly reply. They not only accepted them, but proposed to publish a special small limited edition beside the ordinary edition; and all this in spite of the fact that Dottie Wellesley had decided the year before to give up her sponsorship of the Living Poets series. I date the gradual healing of the wounds caused by my abrupt departure in September 1932 from that moment. Communications, though still rare, were re-established, and the following year I felt bold enough to send Virginia a piece I had written on her imaginative method in *The Waves*; in particular on the way she develops the key images associated with each character in the book. I see now that it was hopelessly inadequate as a study of this side of her technique; but she sent me a very interesting letter in reply, in which she said:

Of course, my attempt was to get that kind of effect, by those means – metaphors, rhythm, repetition as you say – But in actual writing one's mind, as you know, gets into a trance, and the different images seem to come unconsciously. It is very interesting to me, though, to see how deliberate it looks to a critic. Of course most of the work is done before one writes, and the concentration of writing makes one forget what the general effect is.

Meanwhile, Christopher had, inevitably, left Nazified Berlin, and in the middle of May, as he describes in *Christopher and His Kind*, set out for Greece with his new young friend Heinz. It was the beginning of a long odyssey of wanderings from country to country, lasting several years. His chief aim was to find a place where he could work and live with Heinz (an Aryan German and therefore subject to the eventual Nazi call-up when conscription was brought in), for as long as the authorities would grant them a *permis de séjour.* This led him, with occasional flying visits to London, through Greece, the Canary Isles, Paris, Brussels, Copenhagen, Amsterdam and Sintra in Portugal, in a state of perpetual alarm lest war should break out and catch them both abroad, but working very hard all the time on his Berlin books and eventually on the Group Theatre plays he had begun to write with Wystan Auden. Early in 1934 an offer came to him out of the blue (in fact through the agency of the original of Sally Bowles) of just the sort he had long dreamed of: to take part in the direction of the film *Little Friend*, as assistant to the Viennese director Berthold Viertel, an association which was vividly and entertainingly commemorated twelve years later in *Prater Violet*. He took Heinz to London with him, but when his tourist visa ran out, had no option but to allow him to go back to Berlin and his family. He made one further effort to get him to England again, which ended in disaster at Harwich (both he and Heinz appear to have played their cards as badly as possible), with the refusal of the immigration officer to allow Heinz entry, and his return to Germany. Christopher was too much in love with Heinz by that time to find it endurable to live without him, and managed to get him to Amsterdam where he could visit him however briefly in the intervals of film work. Once *Little Friend* was finished, they started on their travels together again.

During all these vicissitudes Christopher and I kept up an engrossing correspondence. I had ceased to be his publisher when I left the Hogarth Press, but I was deeply interested to see what followed *The Memorial*. There was also another scheme in the wind, for while I was with him in Berlin we had begun to talk of the possibility of founding a magazine together.

In July 1934 he wrote to me from the Pavillon Troika in Orotava, Tenerife, to announce that he and Heinz were living

in a little tea-house kept by an Englishman and a German-American. There is a lovely garden here with tropical flowers and trees and I can work pretty well. I think my novel ought definitely to be finished in another month. It will be dreadfully short – I'm afraid not more than

45,000. I wonder if anybody will be prepared to publish a book of that length? When it is finished I shall begin my other Berlin book at once: nearly the whole of it is already written.

Mr Norris Changes Trains, however, turned out in the end to be a good deal longer. A few weeks later he wrote:

Here, amidst the flowers, our Rousseau life goes on. Heinz has just got me to cut off all his hair. He now looks like one of the boys in a Russian film. Every morning we retire to our tables in the banana grove. H. writes letters, making at least ten copies of each. Indeed, calligraphy is dignified by him to the position of an art. One is reminded of the monks in the middle ages. This place is a sort of monastery, anyhow. It is run by a German of the Göring-Roman Emperor type and an Englishman who dyes his hair. The Englishman loathes women so much that he has put a barbed wire entanglement across an opening in the garden wall, to keep them out.

My novel is exactly three quarters done. I hope to finish it on the day War was declared in 1914. It is a sort of glorified shocker; not unlike the productions of my cousin Graham Greene. When it is done and sent off I think I shall leave at once for another island in this group, La Palma. La Palma has the largest extinct crater in the world. The highest peak is called the Mountain of the Boys. It is reputed to be the most beautiful of all the Canary Islands, but is seldom visited.

I wrote and told him that I was sending him a copy of *The Noise of History*. He wrote back from Tenerife, after a tour of the other islands, at the end of August:

Today is my birthday. Thirty years old, with a few white hairs above the ears but still wonderfully preserved, a lonely figure with a typewriter in the midst of a banana grove. . . . I am sorry to have to wait so long for your book. What noise does History make? I imagine something like the loudspeaker at the German café in Orotava, a superhuman bass voice speaking through whistles, crackling and loud pops. What's your long short story about and have you a copy to send me? I starve for my friends' works. . . . Heinz and I remain very happy, except when we think of the future. We hold endless conferences on where to go, what to do, when the smash comes; but arrive nowhere. We are like two frightened rabbits.

Christopher evidently starved for his friends' presence as well as their works. In the same letter he wrote: 'How I wish we could have a huge party: you, Stephen, Wystan, Edward, William, Forster, Rosamond, Beatrix, Wogan, Gerald, the Tonys and Olive Mangeot.' William was, I think, William Plomer; Wogan was my sister Rosamond's second husband, now Lord Milford; Gerald was Gerald Hamilton. One of the Tonys was my Viennese friend, secretary and chauffeur. The other (or others) I am not sure about. As he relates in *Christopher and His Kind*, he had met my sister Beatrix in Berlin and become very much attached to her. They had gone to plays and films together. He had written to me in late December 1932: 'Beatrix is here. I like her most awfully. Yesterday we went to see Faust. Gründgens played Mephistopheles as a sinister sissy and crawled up Faust's waistcoat like a caterpillar. It was an electrifying performance.'

Early in the following year Christopher and Heinz reached Amsterdam again, and invited me to come and stay with them on one of my journeys between Vienna and London. I arrived eventually at the beginning of July, and an event took place which had much to do with my return to working with Leonard and Virginia two years later.

Christopher has told us in his book that there was open-air boxing going on on the sports field, but I seem to remember – perhaps by a distortion of memory – football training. We had gone for a lesiurely stroll on the outskirts of the city, and when we came to whatever the athletic activity was, stopped for quite a long time to discuss and define at last in some detail what had become extremely urgent in my mind and was certainly preoccupying Christopher as well: the magazine we wanted to produce, had talked of so often and had dreamed about for so long. He maintains that he was so captivated by the youthful beauty of the boxers that he hardly heard what I was saying, and agreed to all my suggestions almost without being aware of them. If so, I can only say that he gave a quite wonderfully convincing performance as a deeply attentive listener.

As I have described in *The Whispering Gallery*, I wanted the magazine, first of all, to be international. I believed that there were writers in many countries of Europe who were doing new and exciting work, and whose feelings, especially against the fascism that seemed to be on the point of swamping the whole continent, were similar to ours; they were like us, too, in their desire to bridge the gap between the middle-class, well-educated world and the less articulate, less fortunate, working-class world. In my travels around Europe, I had already got to know many of these writers, and had even dreamed that they could be found in Russia as well. I was still pretty green about the conditions under which Soviet writers worked; but I *did* eventually find one or two who seemed to be worthy to stand with the others from non-totalitarian countries, especially during my trip to the Caucasus in 1936. At the same time I had no intention of choosing writers simply because they were politically acceptable to the anti-fascist Left. I had fairly close connections for a time with *Left Review*, but there it seemed to me that, in the field of imaginative literature which interested me most, politics came, fatally, first. It was a spirit, a near-revolutionary mood of the time that I was after; something anti-mandarin, anti-establishment in both style and outlook, but not tied to a political party or dogma.

In all these rather inchoate aims, I had Christopher's close sympathy. We were also agreed that it was high time that an outlet should be provided in England for long short-stories, the *novella*-length fiction that was easily publishable in France, Germany or Italy, but fell between the stools of the so-called 'full-length' novel, acceptable in England to the circulating libraries, and the short pieces that could be printed in the *London Mercury* or other, more popular, magazines that were open to fiction. Christopher was particularly keen on this, and I feel pretty sure that our decision to aim for that kind of magazine gave him the vital encouragement to break up what remained of *The Lost* into just such long short-stories. In *Christopher and His Kind* he generously makes me responsible 'for the informal form of *Goodbye to Berlin*'. It is certainly agreeable for me to think that my enthusiasm for the various long fragments that eventually made up the book gave him the final push into abandoning *Paul is Alone*, that novel which his subconscious was resisting and of which he only completed a couple of chapters; but a few months before, when he had finished with Wystan Auden the play that was finally to be called *The Dog Beneath the Skin*, he had written to me that after finishing two shorter pieces he planned to 'go on to the second Berlin book, into which all that you missed in Mr Norris will be decanted'. It is of course possible that at that time he intended the second Berlin book to be a connected whole, as he had perhaps implied in the 1932 letter I have quoted earlier.

For some time, in the negotiations with publishers which I immediately entered into when I reached London, it was uncertain whether our magazine would crystallize as a quarterly, or something more like *The Yellow Book*, appearing twice a year in hard covers. Eventually the latter scheme won the day; and eventually the name *New Writing* won against many others that had been mooted.

I wrote at once to Christopher to tell him the glad news:

Your own contribution can be anything between 3,000 and 12,000 words long. However deeply Wystan A. may have involved himself with the Empire-builders and their film-hacks, he must not be allowed to leave for our far-flung territories without producing something. He will probably write it while you stand over him one evening. My homage to him when he comes. I think the moment has arrived for me to write to Edward Upward myself now that you have prepared the way. Can you give me his address? And will you find out from Stephen whether his contribution is finished, or nearly finished? Put the pen in his hand if not. I'm reckoning to be able to pay each contributor (of prose more than 3,000 words in length) at least £4 on account of royalties.

This sounds a very small payment, even for those days; but the Bodley Head (with Allen Lane and Lindsay Drummond in charge) only gave me an advance of £60 for each number, and that had to cover all editorial expenses and translators' fees, as well as contributors'. Needless to say, it was always exceeded; and if it had not been for the indulgent sympathy and support of my mother – whom I was able to pay back in full many years later – *New Writing* would have been on the rocks in a very short time indeed.

I enclosed in my letter to Christopher a draft of the 'Manifesto' I wanted to put in the front of the first number. On 2 September he replied from Amsterdam:

So glad the prospects for *New Writing* are so good. Do you really think paragraph four of your Manifesto is necessary at all? I only ask this tentatively. It seems to me merely the same as saying the 'vital creative work' *will* be vital. And, anyhow, the aims of the paper will be self-evident already in the contents of the first issue. It seems to me that to make any statement of your aims at all lays you open to attacks from the further and hither Left. Surely it is enough to say what you suggest in the other paragraphs and leave the names of the contributors to suggest the nature of the contents?

Originally my idea had been that there should be a kind of advisory committee to assist the editor, but Christopher was doubtful about it. In the same letter he wrote: 'Certainly I will be most honoured to sit on the advisory committee, if you don't think my absence from England disqualifies me? But let me urge you, once more, to take as little notice of us all as possible, and be very autocratic. I'm sure it's better. Need you, in fact, have a formal committee at all? Why not just consult people informally, whenever you want an outside opinion?'

The idea of a committee was dropped. Perhaps, when he urged me to be 'very autocratic', his instinct told him that I was likely to be that anyway; perhaps he felt that, in the restless, wandering life he was leading, it would turn out to be too much of a tie, or just too difficult to keep up. I set to work at once – and there was a great deal to do, especially in wheedling contributions out of foreign authors. I was carried forward on a huge wave of enthusiasm; what I did not fully realize for some time was that what Christopher has called 'John the Poet' was being submerged in that wave.

In October Christopher wrote from Brussels:

> Wystan was here last week-end. He showed me some lyrics and oddments he had written for films, which I liked. And he said you should have them if you wanted them. Although some of them have already appeared in a film called 'Coal-Face', even the producer himself admitted that they were quite inaudible, so unless they are printed they will be lost to mankind. I am getting on with my contribution as fast as I can.

A month later, a postcard arrived: 'The Kulaks are coming, hurrah, hurrah. Hope you'll like them.' This was the original name for the first of the long-short-stories he had worked up out of what remained of *The Lost*, after *Mr Norris* had been given an independent life. I certainly did like this first offering, very much indeed. But very soon after he began to have doubts about the title. On 16 January (1936) he wrote from Sintra:

> About the Kulaks: it occurs to me that maybe, if the book is to be read at all in Russia, the title conveys a quite wrong impression. Do you think I should change the family name? I could do this, of course, in proof: or maybe it could be done before the MS goes to press. What about Nowack? 'The Nowacks' – Nowak is perhaps better. Yes, 'The Nowaks'. (I have just been to ask Heinz, who thinks it can only be spelt Nowack: maybe you could check up on this?)

Curiously enough, his story *was* read in Russia, where it appeared in a little paperback all by itself: HOBAKN. (I have often wondered what the puritans of the Communist Party thought of Otto's ambiguous adventures.) In the same letter Christopher went on:

> What are you writing now? Am very busy on my novel. I will try and do something for number three. There is another section of *The*

Lost ready – about an English girl who sings in a Berlin cabaret, but I hardly think it would suit the serious tone of New Writing. It's rather like Anthony Hope: The Dolly Dialogues. It is an attempt to satirize the romance-of-prostitution racket. Good heter stuff.

This was, of course, the genesis of Sally Bowles. He was not, however, satisfied with it. Before he had seen the first number of *New Writing*, he wrote from Sintra: 'We are all very much excited about New Writing. . . . I'm afraid I couldn't get the proposed story ready in time for the *next* number. It is finished after a fashion but there's something radically wrong with it at present: it must be thought over.' In addition, he wanted to show it to Edward Upward. There was also, he insisted, the necessity of getting the approval of the real-life Sally (Jean Ross).

I no longer remember why we didn't print Wystan's 'Coal-Face' script. He did not appear at all in No. 1, but 'Alfred, a Cabaret Sketch' appeared in No. 2, and in No. 3 the famous and beautiful 'Lay your sleeping-head, my love' – the first of many of his most outstanding poems of the time which first appeared in *New Writing*.

By the end of April, *New Writing* No. 1 had arrived in Sintra. Christopher wrote to me:

I must say, I think it is very handsome and one of the best six shillings-worth I have ever seen. I haven't read everything yet, of course. Yours, which I turned to first, seems admirable. One of your most successful works. . . . I liked also very much Plomer's contribution ['Notes on a visit to Ireland'] and that brilliant story by Chamson ['My Enemy'] which makes one feel that a real artist can write about absolutely anything and still produce all the correct reflections about fascism, nationalism etc. in the reader's mind: a very trite observation, but it always comes as a fresh surprise.

He urged me to publish Edward Upward's *The Railway Accident* in No. 2, as he thought it 'one of the most magnificent pieces of narrative prose produced since the war', and would need very little bowdlerization; but this plan fell through, chiefly I seem to remember owing to the author's reluctance (I had published a section from his novel *Journey to the Border* in the first number). And he went on: 'Look here, if you'd like some stuff for Number Two, I could send you some of my Berlin Diary. About five thousand words. But don't have it if you don't want. It is only mildly (heter) dirty and chiefly about my landlady, fellow-lodgers, pupils, etc.'

I did want it, but the problems of the longer story had to be settled first. It was not till October that he wrote to me in Vienna from London: ' "Sally Bowles" has unexpectedly passed Edward Upward – so I am sending it to you. If you like it and want to publish, we must somehow get the consent of the original, who is at present abroad, otherwise the risk of an action is too great for us to take.'

As far as I was concerned, the risk of libel action was not the only problem about the story. I was fascinated by it, and certainly did not think it too frivolous for our magazine; but it was long, too long I thought even for *New Writing*; worse, I was worried about the abortion episode, and wondered whether, in the climate of those days, our printers would pass it. I explained my doubts to Christopher. He wrote back from Brussels in January 1937:

About SALLY, you know I'm doubtful, though quite open to conviction. It seems to me that Sally, without the abortion sequence, would just be a silly little capricious bitch. Besides, what would the whole thing lead up to? And down from? The whole idea of the study is to show that even the greatest disasters leave a person like Sally essentially unchanged.... Surely the less pretentious Berlin Diary is really a much better bit of work?

After this letter I luckily gave up the rather half-hearted attempt to persuade Christopher to cut Sally, and published the 'Berlin Diary' in No. 3. Meanwhile, however, Jean Ross had given her permission, and *Sally Bowles* was eventually published, with what struck me as considerable courage, in its little separate book by Leonard and Virginia at the Hogarth Press.

During the course of the next twelve months Christopher seemed as happy as I was about the success of *New Writing*, and the new authors it had attracted to itself. We had already published in No. 2 George Orwell's 'Shooting an Elephant', V. S. Pritchett's 'You Make Your Own Life' ('The Sailor' was to come later), and Rex Warner's 'The Football Match' (an extract from 'The Wild Goose Chase'); and from abroad in addition to Chamson we had Silone, Giono, Olyesha, Pasternak, Brecht and Lorca among our contributors. With vital help from Stephen, we were collecting a number of beautiful Spanish poems inspired by the Civil War for our autumn number 1937. Christopher set himself to the task of exploring for new contributors and chivvying some of the English poets, Wystan, Stephen, Louis MacNeice, when I was out of range. We had at first deliberately kept poetry to a minimum – No. 1 had only four poems by Stephen (of which three were translations from Hölderlin) and a translation of Pasternak's long and famous poem (*1905*), as we felt that Geoffrey Grigson's *New Verse* provided the poets of our generation with a satisfying outlet; but as time went on they began to gravitate towards *New Writing*, and we published an increasing proportion of poetry, notably some of Louis's as well as Wystan's most impressive work. Christopher had also brought off a much appreciated coup in persuading E. M. Forster to let us have a piece about the Paris International Exhibition, which was called 'The Last Parade'. He sent it to me in August:

Here is Morgan's exhibition piece. One of the best, I think, he has ever written. We can be proud that *New Writing* has secured it. He has only this partial typescript. So I typed out the sheets in duplicate and am sending them off at once to Lawrence & Wishart. They will have them by the afternoon post. . . . Wystan and my plans remain distracted and vague. W. wants to stay in England to save money, but there seems no particular place to go. Maybe we shall come [to Vienna] after all. I am very bothered. And the film people are being tiresome beyond description. And so are Fabers. And so is the Group Theatre. If only you were in Vienna and could say: this costs so much and so much. Sorry to be so floppy. I am still up to the ears in little tasks.

New Writing had transferred from the Bodley Head to Lawrence & Wishart at the end of the contract with the former, which was for three numbers. The Bodley Head let us drop, not because of lack of sales or general interest, but because a sudden crisis had exploded in their midst with the departure of Allen Lane, the dynamo of the whole business, to found Penguin Books. Everything seemed at sixes and sevens in Bury Street, and the kindly, charming Lindsay Drummond was too nervous of the future to sign a new contract. Lawrence & Wishart got wind of what was happening, and made overtures; they had the poet Edgell Rickword, whom I had always admired, as one of their chief editorial advisers, and I think he was responsible for pushing the contract through, again for three numbers. They were of course attracted by the left-wing slant of the enterprise. I don't think I was aware at the time how close their ties were with the Communist Party; but I have to say that they left me entire editorial freedom, and behaved with the most scrupulous tact. That they too lost interest after the three numbers they had committed themselves to was, I suppose, due to their tardy realization that I had the most obstinate and tiresome determination to go my own way as a chooser of contributors and contributions, especially as the political complexities of the Spanish War developed. Nevertheless I have nothing but gratitude to them for the rescue operation at a very ticklish moment.

Soon after Christopher had written his rather desperate letter about the confusion of his plans for the future, he and Wystan spent a few weeks in Dover with E. M. Forster, William Plomer and their friends. The projected visit to Vienna, which I would so much have welcomed, was definitely off, because while in Dover they had more or less decided to go to the Far East, accepting a commission from Fabers to write a book about the Sino-Japanese War. Since the fiasco of the attempt, through

Gerald Hamilton, to get Heinz a Mexican passport, and the disaster of his arrest as soon as he recrossed the German frontier – ostensibly to arrange a further visa for staying in Belgium – Christopher had no further special ties to keep him in Europe.

On 15 September 1937 he wrote to me:

If possible, I want to get the new play, 'On the Frontier', produced before Christmas. Then there is the 'North-West Passage' which I finished this morning: it will mean a lot of interviews and proof-correcting and what not. Then I'd like, if possible, to write all the remaining fragments of 'The Lost' before we sail, so that my Berlin life is finally tidied up, all ready to be audited before the Judgement Seat. You shall certainly have some of it for 'New Writing'.

What he did in fact get ready for me, just before the departure for China, was *The Landauers*. The 'North-West Passage' had its title changed to *Lions and Shadows* and was published by the Hogarth Press in 1938.

As I have described earlier on, some degree of communication with Leonard and Virginia had already been re-established by 1935, and indignation and injury on both sides had faded with time. In addition my deep-seated urge to follow a career in publishing, if I had to follow any career at all, had not been extinguished. By 1937 I had at least a hunch that Lawrence & Wishart were not going to renew their contract after the spring 1938 number had gone to press. I was, therefore, already looking for a new home for my child. A little bird – or rather several little birds – had whispered in my ear that if I made renewed advances to the Woolfs, they would not be unwelcome. Also, at the back of my mind was still the idea of making *New Writing* the centre of actual book publishing for the works of our generation. I had not succeeded in selling this idea to Lawrence & Wishart. Much more likely with the Hogarth Press, as before. After all, Christopher was still on their list.

In his autobiography Leonard asserts that he never had any

intention of selling the Hogarth Press *as a whole* to me or to anyone else. But in this matter, as in so many other points of detail in the last, posthumously published volume of that remarkable work, his memory betrayed him. The facts (as I have since carefully checked them) are that just at the time when I was beginning to look for a new home for *New Writing*, he and Virginia had come to the conclusion that the Press was becoming an intolerable burden to them. They despaired at last of finding the ideal Manager – or Manager-victim as I have sometimes thought – and wanted to sell the entire business to someone who would be in sympathy with its character and previous history, and who would keep it going on much the same lines.

It was just at this point that I reappeared, and went to see them. They put their predicament before me at once. Very much elated, I asked them to name a figure. Leonard suggested £6,000, and in the letter in which he proposed this sum, went on to say:

In any case I should wish to give up all business control. . . . We should be prepared to retain an advisory interest. It would of course be impossible to obtain a binding legal indefinite agreement that Virginia and Vita would continue to publish with you. All one can say is that their agreements would stand exactly as they do today with the Press, namely that they will submit their next books. As regards Virginia, I can say definitely that one of the reasons why we would rather that the Press continued in its present form with some connection remaining with us rather than that we should sell it to be absorbed by a large publisher is that she would like to publish with it.

Unfortunately, I could not find as much as £6,000 – which I suppose is the equivalent of something between £40,000 and £50,000 at the time I am writing. Various persons were suggested who might come in with me, but for one reason or another they were eliminated. Then a terrible disaster occurred. In the middle of July the Woolfs heard that their nephew, my friend Julian Bell who had gone out to Spain to drive an ambulance, had been killed. 'The news came last night,' Leonard wrote to me. 'There is nothing to be said except about the sheer waste and futility of it all. It is the war all over again, when one was rung up to be told that Rupert was dead, or one's brother killed, and one knew that it was only in order to produce the kind of world we are living in now. Horrible.'

At the same time Julian's younger brother Quentin, to whom I had long been devoted, wrote to me: 'I'm afraid I have frightfully bad news, Julian has been killed on the Madrid front, all we know is that he died of wounds. I don't know what to say and now really can't say more. I know how you'll feel. All my love to you.'

This shattering news made us all feel we had better drop the negotiations for a while: they were in any case deadlocked. By the beginning of October the Woolfs had decided that they would have to let the Press 'die off', refusing all new books and just keeping it for their own books. This was a decision of despair; but, soon after, Leonard nevertheless had the sudden idea that he would approach me again with the suggestion that I and the rest of what he called 'the young Brainies', that is Stephen Spender, Christopher Isherwood and Wystan Auden, should buy the Press and run it collectively, with myself as Manager.

I liked the suggestion, and immediately did what I could to sound the others. No good: it soon became evident that they were not in a position to produce that necessary half of the money required. When I told Leonard and Virginia this, I also told them that I was still ready to stump up £3,000 for my own part. They had further thoughts, and in the end did decide that they would sell a half share to me alone for that sum. In theory this share would be Virginia's, and she would technically retire from the Press. It was on this new basis that an agreement was finally concluded.

It came into force at the beginning of April 1938; though, curiously, it was dated 19 May, I can no longer remember why. After signing, I wrote to Virginia:

Leonard was very rugged the other day when I signed the Partnership Agreement, and to my proposal that the event be marked by a mutual health-drinking, replied that he only had cold water. Never-

theless I refuse to be dashed, and think that at any rate I owe you a
letter, in which joy at reaching such an honourable position in such a
distinguished and old established firm is mixed with tears for the
departure from the same position of its co-founder and chief literary
glory. No doubt it is long habitation in Vienna that's taught me to be
so flowery and courteous, because, as you have reminded me, I was
pretty severe in the old days. . . . No, but seriously, I hope the new
arrangement is going to release you and Leonard for a steady stream of
masterpieces. I stand with both hands extended, waiting for them.

To this letter Virginia replied on the 22 April 1938: 'I'm full of
sanguinity about the future; and thankful to lift the burden on
to your back. Nor can I see myself any reason why we should
quarrel; or why we should drink the Toast in cold water. What
about a good dinner (not English) at Boulestin or some such place?
You are hereby invited to be the guest of Virginia Woolf's
ghost – the Hogarth ghost: who rises let us hope elsewhere.'
Leonard himself wrote afterwards to say: 'I am sorry that I was
"gruff" over the signature of the agreement, and I certainly did
not grudge you a glass of wine. It was emotion!' To my regret,
I cannot remember anything about the Boulestin dinner. Perhaps
because the liquid in which the Toast was drunk was abundant –
and definitely not cold water.
I wanted to tell Christopher immediately that at last everything was properly fixed up, but he was on his way back from
China with Wystan. I had to wait until they arrived in London
in the middle of July. Very soon after their return, he came to stay
with me at Totland Bay on the Isle of Wight, where I was spending a few weeks with my mother. The scene was as nostalgic for
him as for me. In long walks over the heather downs, we discussed everything in the world that interested us, and above all of
course new plans for the Hogarth Press and *New Writing*, and the
problem of the title to give the Berlin book. On the first evening,
when we came to the topmost point, from which we could
glimpse Alum Bay and the Needles far down below us in the
gathering twilight, it was eerie to see the barbed-wire fences up

by the old Napoleonic forts, the aeroplanes, the swinging search-lights and the mysterious coloured lamps on the water. We made a joke of it, inventing an absurd spy story to suit what was all around us; but war seemed all the same unexpectedly and un-comfortably close.

The next morning, pacing up and down the tiny lawn in front of the house, with a glimpse of the Solent through the trees, he began telling me about his experiences in China. I took him out to the cliff's edge and made him pose for photographs, with the foam way below just visible in the finder. A broad grin splitting his face, he looked absurdly chubby-cheeked and schoolboyish. They promised to be the best photographs I ever took of him; but they were all ruined in the developing.

Christopher had always had a quite extraordinary gift for describing – in detail – books that he had not only not finished, but sometimes not even begun. I remember him doing just this, in a bar in Antwerp a year or two before, with the scenario of the never-to-be-concluded novel *Paul is Alone* (which he describes in *Christopher and His Kind*). I was enthralled then; and I was en-thralled again on this occasion, as we walked over the downs, by his precise description of another novel (or was it a trilogy?) he planned to write about his years of exile with Heinz. I have some-times wondered whether this gift for seeing a story so vivid and luminous in all its details before he puts pen to paper, has not sometimes made him feel bored when it comes to the actual process of writing. It would account for his comparatively small output of fiction apart from those books so largely composed from his diary notes. Nothing, so far as I know, was ever heard again of the Heinz novel; but at least we have his vivid and poignant account of the whole affair in *Christopher and His Kind*, while bits of the saga appear, transmogrified, here and there in *Down There on a Visit*.

The new situation at the Press made him redouble his efforts to get the Woolfs to publish Edward Upward's novel *Journey to the Border*. Before the end of November he wrote to me:

Edward's book is being published by the Hogarth in early spring. This after a terrific putsch on my part. There was a wonderful dinner party given by the Woolfs to the Upwards, a great success. Virginia is really the nicest woman I know: she was so nice to Mrs. U. Elizabeth Bowen came in afterwards, so Edward got a real glimpse of Blooms- bury, and quite enjoyed it, in his chilly way.

As an earnest of my new hopes, I asked him and Stephen to appear as assistant editors on the title page of the New Series of *New Writing* volumes now to be published by the Hogarth Press, starting in the autumn of 1938; but, though I couldn't realize it at the time, the journey to the Far East was really the beginning of the end of our close collaboration, at any rate in that most productive phase. In China he found a British Ambassador (Sir Archibald Clark-Kerr, later in Washington as Lord Inverchapel) who was an ardent admirer of *Sally Bowles*, and he wrote from Hongkong at the end of February 1938:

Am longing to see *New Writing*. Could a copy come out here? This address holds certainly till the end of May, if not later. And thank you so much for collating the typescripts of the 'Lost' stories. I still don't know if America has taken the book; only that Harper's Bazaar has offered to make Sally Bowles into a serial. Do keep me posted on all the latest Hogarth Press and Daylight developments. If I am killed in China, I'd like my name on the notepaper just the same, with a cute little black cross against it. . . . Delighted to hear that Electra is doing well. Give Peggy my dearest love. I hear from another source that Viertel is going to produce Rosamond's play. Another thing we'll miss!

My sister Beatrix (Peggy) was at that time achieving one of the greatest triumphs of her career in the London production of Eugene O'Neill's *Mourning Becomes Electra*. No one who saw her performance will, I believe, ever be able to forget it. It had such an overwhelming effect on my mother when I took her to see it, that she fainted in the middle and had to be carried out of the auditorium. Berthold Viertel did in fact direct Beatrix in Rosamond's play *No More Music* when it was put on as a Sunday

play early in 1938. It had no luck with the commercial manage-
ments: one of the chief reasons was that, by an altogether extraordinary and disastrous coincidence, Noël Coward had at exactly
the same time written a play with the same name – and the same
Caribbean background.

It was on their return from China through America that
Christopher and Wystan decided that they would like to live in
the USA in future – if they could. I think very few of their intimate
friends realized this. I certainly didn't, though I was aware that
they planned to make another visit in 1939. Even to the last
Christopher hesitated to admit to me that they might be going
there for good. In the section of *Down There on a Visit* called
'Waldemar', which, in spite of certain fictional rearrangements
(there never was a Waldemar in his life), is a fairly accurate
account of his experiences in London at the time of the Munich
crisis, there are indeed hints of a secret resolve being formed; but
it was secret from me too, though I figure fairly intimately in the
story – and in any case 'Waldemar' was published long after. At
the same time I had a warning, though I didn't take it seriously
when it happened. We were on a walk together, somewhere near
the Gray's Inn Road one afternoon, when the news of the sell-out
of the Czechs came through in the evening papers. As we de-
voured them I said bitterly to him: 'Well, that's the end of
Europe as we wanted it!' His answer was to exclaim: 'That
doesn't matter any more to me – I shall be in America.' This
seemed to me to be said so completely without reflection that I
paid little attention to it, forgot to question him, and only
remembered when he had finally gone.

The decision was all the more of a shock to me when I tumbled
to it, because during a year's end trip to Brussels he had written:
'I do think you could lighten your work, and incidentally rub
several people up the right way, if you threw the weight of more
decisions on the shoulders of the advisory board. After all, we
have our uses, if only as an alibi.' So it came about that the last
thing I could do in the collaboration that had been so intimate

and had meant so much to me was to publish those collated type-scripts as *Goodbye to Berlin*: all the pieces *New Writing* had printed, together with *Sally Bowles*, 'On Ruegen Island' and the second 'Berlin Diary'. The book came out in England in March 1939, and was an immediate success; but it was a flop in America at first, and nobody except a handful of discerning people over there listened to Christopher until John Van Druten made his play, *I Am a Camera*, out of it.

Before I resumed my role as Manager – and now Partner as well – at the Hogarth Press, I had decided in any case to wind up my life in Vienna. I had been present when Hitler overran Austria, and saw at once that my life there couldn't go on. I spent much of the summer packing up my belongings in the already Nazified city, making my sad goodbyes, and arranging for my friend Toni and his wife to take over my flat.

The era of Tavistock Square was also coming to an end. Leonard's lease was falling in in the near future, and the landlords had plans for rebuilding. Early in 1939 he found a house, No. 37 Mecklenburgh Square, which appealed to him and Virginia and to me too. By some curious process of osmosis, the firm of solicitors who had shared the house in Tavistock Square had become inseparable from them, and took the same part of the new house as in the old. The move took place in the summer, and in fact had hardly finished before war broke out. Instead of being immured again in the basement, where the rest of the Hogarth Press was established, I was given a room on the ground floor and felt a quite dizzy sense of promotion. The year before, I had taken a flat for myself a few doors down on the same (north) side of the Square, which remained my home until the bombing of September 1940 drove us all out. At the time, it seemed a very satisfactory arrangement in every way for the new start we were all making.

PART III

A NEW START –
AND A NEW WAR

LEONARD was at that time fifty-eight, rather more than a year older than Virginia, well preserved though his lean and narrow face (which always reminded me of a Red Indian chief) was heavily lined. His energy was still formidable. He not only ran the Hogarth Press, but wrote books and a great deal of (mainly political) journalism, was influential on various committees behind the scenes in the Labour Party, and edited the *Political Quarterly*. He was also, when in the country, a zealous gardener.

I was very close to Leonard while I was at the Press, and when, after the break-up of our partnership in 1946 friendly relations were restored, spent evenings and weekends with him on a number of occasions. Nevertheless, he remains to me an enigma: even now I cannot quite fit the different manifestations of his nature into a coherent picture. In his book, *A Boy at the Hogarth Press*, Richard Kennedy has reproduced a drawing he made of Leonard sitting in the front office, with Lord Olivier (author of *The Anatomy of African Misery*) beside him. They are gravely and imperturbably discussing problems of colonial politics, while a shelf above them, which Kennedy had just put up, collapses, showering them with advertising leaflets like a snowstorm. . . . That was one side of Leonard. In disasters and emergencies he could remain calm and resigned, the Roman stoic, as I have already described. But there is another drawing in Kennedy's book, showing Leonard in a towering rage because he had discovered a small error in the petty cash, the day-to-day accounts. That was equally typical of the other side of his nature: an over-developed meticulousness about small details of finance, orderly accounting, and punctuality that seemed quite unworthy of the Cambridge Apostle. Angus Davidson, who stayed longer than anyone else as Manager (though never allowed to express an opinion about the manuscripts) before my arrival, has told us

that if he was two or three minutes late – according to Leonard –
in arriving at the Press in the mornings, he would find him 'fum-
ing, a bundle of papers in hand, looking at his watch'. This spirit
of meticulousness runs right through the later volumes of his
autobiography; and indeed his calculations of the income and
expenditure of himself and Virginia year by year reach a point of
absurdity at which they become weirdly fascinating, adding a
peculiarly original flavour to the work. At the same time I
have to say that it must have been very tedious for Virginia to
live under the supervision of minute calculations so alien to her
nature.

I have always thought that this meticulousness came from the
fact that he grew up in a large middle-class but by no means well-
heeled family where, after the death of his father, an eminent
Victorian QC, every halfpenny counted; and was reinforced by
his years as a colonial administrator in a remote part of Ceylon,
with the severe eyes of the Treasury always upon him. It has,
however, been suggested to me that it was a way of controlling,
or deflecting the powerful and largely frustrated passions that ran
just below the rational surface.

There is no doubt whatsoever in my mind that he was entirely
devoted to the task, to what he considered his duty, of protecting
Virginia from everything that could threaten her mental health,
or disturb her creative work. She, for her part, though she would
sometimes tease him, or pretend to slip away from his watchful
surveillance, was entirely dependent on him. Their bonds were
very close indeed, as anyone who had observed them together
would testify; even so, it must have come as a surprise to some of
their intimate friends to read the letters to him from Virginia,
while she was away in France with Vita, so full of lovers' baby-
talk and animal nicknames. If he sustained her morale by his
appreciation of each of her new books – as she handed the typescript to him before anyone else saw it – there were also occasions
when the traffic went the other way. I remember one autumn
evening at Rodmell, just after I had read *Barbarians at the Gate*,

when I told Leonard how much I had been moved by the lucidity and persuasive force of the argument he developed in that book, and his all too timely warning of the danger of allowing oneself to believe that any means were justified by the ends. Virginia was splashing gravy in large dollops over my plate as I spoke, and joined in with her emphatic praise. 'You know, Leo, it's a *wonderful* book', while Leonard himself sat at the table in modest silence, with lowered eyes, like a schoolboy praised by the headmaster at an end-of-term prize-giving.

I have, however, never been quite sure how much he cared, apart from Virginia, about other human beings. Perhaps he was frightened by the emotions they aroused in him: intense desire for friendship, lust and love, jealousy and the impulse to destroy. The only one among his men friends I am fairly certain he was sincerely attached to was Lytton Strachey, with whom he corresponded regularly and intimately while he was in Ceylon. I never heard, nor can I find, any cutting or dismissive remark made by him about Lytton, though plenty about the other Apostles of his Cambridge – and later Bloomsbury – circle. Of course he had not become a misogynist: he was always attracted by pretty young women and would make himself especially charming to them. Nor do I believe he was insensible to youthful male beauty. He suggests somewhere, casually, almost as an aside, that at Trinity he was in love with 'the Goth', Virginia's elder brother Thoby who died so young. On one occasion, during the middle years of the war, we drove into Lewes together, and I spied a copy of Donatello's nude bronze statue of David in an antique shop. When I pointed it out to him, he was so taken with it that he immediately went in and bought it without haggling. It still adorns his Monk's House garden. And I remembered at the time that in the early months of the war I took a friend to see him and Virginia at Monk's House, a naturally good-looking young man who was even more good looking in the kilted officer's uniform which he had just assumed. Though pleased, I was I admit surprised at the way Leonard immediately put himself out for him, engaged him in interested conversation, and exercised all his charm upon him.

He was, in any case, very fond of animals. In the years I knew him, he owned a succession of spaniels, who were scarcely ever away from him, however filthy they became in country walks. At one period he also owned a marmoset, which I remember sitting on his knee and chattering with rage at me – almost shaking its tiny fist at me – during our editorial discussions; evidently considering my proximity a threat to its master. In *Downhill All the Way* Leonard tells an amusing story of how Mitz acted as a kind of charm for them when they took her on a car tour of the Continent in 1935, reducing grim stormtroopers in Hitler's Reich to gooey rapture. She died just before Christmas in 1938.

In spite of what I have said, I have an uncomfortable feeling that Leonard did in the end infect Virginia to a certain degree with his own attitude towards money. There is an unpleasant (to me) entry in Virginia's diary, which I saw while I was preparing this book, about a visit to my mother's house in Bourne End for luncheon soon after I had rejoined the Press. My mother, who was not at all well off at that time but was still just managing to keep up Fieldhead, naturally put the best of the inherited family silver out for the occasion. When they drove away, the two visitors apparently said to one another that it was clear that my mother lived in great style and they ought to have asked more than £3,000 for my partnership in the Press.

Of course Virginia had every right to be concerned about the capital value and earnings of the Press. After the earliest years, the profits from her books were the major element in keeping it prosperous, and attractive as a business proposition to a potential partner. Under the curious arrangement she and Leonard had come to in the first period of their marriage, all earnings of both of them, whether from the Hogarth Press or their own writings, were pooled. Out of this pool first came their expenses, and then they divided the rest fifty-fifty (or so one must assume from what

Leonard tells us) a plan which as time went on must have favoured him more and more. The expenses included the gradual rebuilding and embellishment of Monk's House. One can see from Virginia's letters what pleasure it gave her when the good sales of one of her books, *Orlando* for instance which put her finally in the best-seller class, made it possible to add another bathroom, or lavatory, or even living room to the little rambling house which had been so ill equipped with civilized amenities when they first bought it.

My return to the Press meant that the visits to Monk's House, which I had enjoyed so much during my 1931-2 apprenticeship, were resumed. Now that I was a Partner, discussions about manuscripts which had been submitted to us occupied a good deal more of the time during these visits. Nevertheless, we generally relaxed after dinner in the upstairs sitting room, where the shelves were filled with books which Virginia had re-bound for herself in bright paper covers, and the tables covered with current weeklies and monthlies in the midst of which Leonard had placed some of his choicest pot-plants, on whose nurture in his greenhouse he prided himself so much: double begonias with their huge rosette heads of brilliant scarlet, yellow and white, almost too heavy for their fleshy stems, gloxinias and heavily perfumed lilies. Leonard would puff at the pipe that was always going out, Virginia would light another home-rolled cigarette in her long holder, and we began the endless gossip that delighted Virginia so much, about mutual friends and acquaintances and Hogarth authors past and present. I enjoyed drawing Virginia out about famous writers she had known, and the circles of her girlhood, but I don't think my curiosity was a patch on hers. In particular, she longed to hear details of the sexual lives of my generation, and would cross-question me pertinac ously.

I remember one evening when she opened the conversation: 'Now, John, tell us about your bugger-boys.' This sudden direct approach did not, of course, fail to embarrass me. I decided quickly not to talk about Vienna as too many explanations would have been needed to give her a picture of my way of life there, where passionate friendships were mixed up with political or semi-political activity, but instead told her about a drummer called Fred, an amiable and amusing adolescent in one of the Guards regiments who had been my friend a year or two before. I explained to her as best I could that it was not unusual for people of my tastes to choose a friend in the Guards; the relationship had a mercenary basis, yes, but the young men were at that time generally reliable and even affectionate (certainly in the case of Fred who developed guilt complexes later about leaving me in the lurch), though it was wise not to kid oneself that one was the only recipient of their favours.

'But does this really go on all the time in London?' Virginia exclaimed. 'Leo, have you ever heard of it?' Leonard took his pipe out of his mouth, and replied with judicious gravity: 'Yes, oh yes. It's been going on ever since anyone can remember. What can one expect when the soldiers are so badly paid? Not at all unusual.' Virginia digested this addition to her knowledge about the *mores* of London in silence for some minutes. I doubt if she was in the least shocked; she had known about inversion from her early Bloomsbury days, and had a number of close friends, Lytton Strachey above all, who made no secret of their inclinations, though this particular aspect of the life appeared to be new to her. She had in any case asked for it; and it didn't alter her attitude towards me in any way at all.

One of the first books I had to deal with was the memorial volume to Julian, which came out as *Julian Bell: Essays, Poems and Letters.* I was not happy with it: it seemed to me altogether too bulky a volume – nearly four hundred pages – to inveigle the attention of the reading public towards someone who, outstandingly gifted, admired by all his friends, and lovable though he was, had scarcely made any impact outside Cambridge when he died. Ostensibly it was edited by his brother Quentin, but a great many other cooks managed to get their spoons into the broth, including J. M. Keynes, E. M. Forster, Charles Mauron, and David Garnett who was given the task of selecting from Julian's large correspondence, and in the end chose eighty letters, which took up 175 pages. Quentin's own voice in fact, amid the babble of the others, was not heard at all, – a fact I very much regretted. Surely a memoir by him, I thought, of about sixty or seventy thousand words, quoting fairly fully from his letters and poems, would have been fairer to Julian's memory and more likely to appeal to a wider public than this Bloomsbury Monument? It was expensive to produce and difficult to sell. Vanessa was very anxious to get my approval, but I was too late on the scene to have any influence. A far more effective tribute was produced thirty years later by William Abrahams and Peter Stansky in *Journey to the Frontier*.

I started my new career as Partner in the Hogarth Press with high hopes that the old days of altercation with Leonard were over; but in the sixteen months up to the outbreak of war our relations once more began to deteriorate, and there were moments when I was reduced to something near despair when contemplating the future, though of course my position was far stronger than it had been in 1931 and 1932. The chief bone of contention was *New Writing*. A new series was started when it came over to the Hogarth Press, and the first number was published in the autumn of 1938, and a second in the spring of 1939; but already before that the wrangling had started. Leonard, it soon became clear, did not like *New Writing* and wanted to clip its wings, on the ground that though the reviews were still very good it was not making money. I, however, believed that sooner or later it would make money (and in this belief I was justified), and that meanwhile it should be considered as a publication which brought considerable prestige and acted as a magnet for a new generation of writers. When Leonard and I had our preliminary discussions, I was fully under the impression that he appreciated this. Hadn't one of the main reasons for my approaching him and Virginia again been that I was looking for a new home for it? More precisely, in the

letters we exchanged at the beginning of 1938, I had made it
perfectly clear that one of the conditions I assumed were agreed
between us was (I quote from my letter of 15 January): 'that
either of us has an absolute veto on any book proposed to be
published by the other, though it is in advance agreed that the
works of yourself and Virginia and future numbers of *New
Writing* . . . shall be undertaken by us.' At the time Leonard in no
way dissented from this interpretation of our relationship-to-be
in the Press. Nevertheless, in January 1939, announcing that he
was thinking of exercising his right of veto on No. 2, he said
flatly that 'the publication of N.W. was not a condition of your
entering the Press. All conditions from your side were put in
writing, and this was not one of them.' He claimed afterwards
that he had not been able to find my letter of 15 January, but my
immediate, and I think understandable, reaction was that he was
trying to double-cross me on an issue he knew was particularly
sensitive, and to evade the whole spirit of the partnership. I
fought him bitterly. In the end the row was settled by my
agreeing, for the sake of peace, to take a small cut in the small
advance the Press was paying me.

This was not the only clash that took place in those early
months, and I poured out my feelings of disillusionment and
dismay to Christopher who was in Brussels with Wystan in
December 1938. He wrote back:

I'm afraid your life at Tavistock Square must be very difficult
indeed. I don't wonder you sometimes get rattled. But there is no help
for it. A publisher must be tactful, and yet more tactful – yes, to the
very end. . . . At the same time, I do think you could lighten your
work, and incidentally, rub several people up the right way, if you
threw the weight of more decisions on to the shoulders of the advisory
board. After all, we have our uses, if only as an alibi. For instance, you
could send Wystan more poetry. And you could send me more novels.
. . . You know we are only too glad of any chance to co-operate, and I
sometimes feel you wouldn't feel yourself so isolated in your struggle
with the Other Partner if you appealed to the board more often.

Stephen, I'm sure, would respond to this policy very warmly. What he really wants is to feel that he's being useful.

Touched as I was by this offer, I felt a certain irritation too. Christopher seemed to be dreaming and pretending to me about the possibility of us all working together. Ever since the return from China he had seemed withdrawn into obscure preoccupations which he shared only with Wystan. His letter would have struck me as even odder if I had had an inkling that what he was debating with Wystan was a final departure for America. I answered rather tartly:

How, may I ask, are you to lighten my work of reading at the Press, if you use England rather as I use my Club? A few weeks a year you seem to be available, and then off on the great trek again. But would-be Hogarth authors know no close season, nor do their beaters, the agents. . . . Of course I'd like you and Wystan and all to read and advise more, and you mustn't imagine for a moment it's because I don't trust you. Stephen, for instance, can do really brilliant poetry reports. The simple fact is, not merely that you're rarely to be found, but that people must (and most certainly should) be rewarded for reading work, and the H.P. just can't afford a heavy overhead on this item.

In spite of these exchanges, manuscripts did from time to time cross the Channel between Brussels and London. In particular, poems submitted to us were sent over to Wystan, and came back with amusing and characteristically shrewd comments. 'I sometimes think that Hopkins ought to be kept on a special shelf like a dirty book, and only be allowed to readers who won't be ruined by him,' he wrote in criticizing one young poet's work. An occasional novel that had excited my special interest was also sent to Christopher. 'I believe I've found a really first-class novel. I long for you to read it,' I wrote to him in the same letter as I had let myself go about my situation at the Press. 'L. hasn't pronounced yet.' This was the manuscript of Henry Green's *Party Going*, which his close friend Goronwy Rees had persuaded him to send me. He had already written two novels, a youthful tour-de-force,

Blindness, which he had begun while at school at Eton, followed by *Living,* a work of totally unusual but undoubted genius based on his experiences as a learner in his family's engineering works. It had failed to achieve more than a *succès d'estime,* and his publishers had shown a marked lack of enthusiasm about the new novel. Discouraged, he had let it lie in a bottom drawer until urged to send it to me. The pattern of Christopher and *The Memorial* was repeating itself in an extraordinary way. I sent the manuscript to Christopher a week or two later, and wrote: 'I'm longing to hear what you have to say about Henry Green's MS, which I have just sent you. I – and many others – think it is an amazing bit of work.' Christopher agreed emphatically; and after Leonard and Virginia had expressed very much the same kind of doubts as they had in the case of *The Memorial,* it was accepted by the Press and published in 1939, with a strikingly original jacket by John Banting, whom I had already introduced to design a jacket for *The Memorial.*

The arrival of Henry Green as a Hogarth author seemed to me to start a new phase, and gave me confidence for the future. He had never been associated with the left-wing intellectual movement of the thirties, and yet in *Living* he seemed to have solved, without any political undertones, many of the problems that had exercised us about 'proletarian' writing. I felt that a new momentum was gathering, leading me to turn my gaze, still lingering on the backward scene, towards the discoveries of the future. During the war Henry produced in rapid succession a series of brilliant books, more than justifying our belief in him. He also became a much-treasured friend, vivacious and endlessly witty and amusing.

It was also rewarding to be able to publish in the same year Tom Hopkinson's novel *The Man Below.* Tom, who was then assistant editor on *Weekly Illustrated* and was very soon to become famous as one of the founder-editors of *Picture Post,* had sent me an extraordinarily original short story, 'I Have Been Drowned', which I printed in *New Writing* No. 3. It was most graphic and imaginatively convincing; I was utterly astonished to learn, when I met him, that though obsessed by boats he had never experienced near-drowning, except in fantasy.

By the time *Party Going* came out Christopher and Wystan had already left for America, leaving my foolish self still unaware that they were going with the strong inclination to stay there if they liked it, and become American citizens. To help them with the money for this journey, they had proposed to write a joint travel book for the Hogarth Press, on the lines of *Journey to a War*, to be called *Address Not Known*. Then they decided that this plan was a mistake, but as Wystan badly needed money a business meeting was arranged between us, with Christopher as stage manager, during which he agreed to let the Hogarth Press have his next book of poems, in return for a much needed cheque which I produced out of my own small *New Writing* funds, to avoid involving Leonard at that stage. He assured me that he was free to make this commitment, and my fingers almost trembled with excitement as I signed the cheque. Unfortunately, when the time came to deliver the manuscript of the volume originally called *The Double Man*, but published as *New Year Letter*, Tom Eliot pointed out that Wystan was bound by contract to Faber, in spite of what he had asserted. In the end we had an amicable lunch together, and Tom generously reimbursed me for the financial advance I had made. Wystan's contribution to the crisis was neither to send apologies nor excuses, but a telegram from New York: 'I am incapable of dealing with this.'

Apart from one or two brief postcards and letters, I did not hear from Christopher until the beginning of May, when he was about to leave New York for the West Coast:

As soon as I'm in Hollywood, I plan to write a piece for you about New York. I have quite a lot to say about it. Oh God, what a city! The nervous breakdown expressed in terms of architecture. The skyscrapers are all Father-fixations. The police-cars are fitted with air-raid sirens, specially designed to promote paranoia. The elevated railway is the circular madness. The height of the buildings produces visions similar to those experienced by Ransom in F.6.

In the same letter, he made a surprising but crucial confession:

I myself am in the most Goddamawful mess. I have discovered, what I didn't realize before, or what I wasn't till now, that I am a pacifist. And now I have to find out what that means, and what duties it implies. That's one reason why I am going out to Hollywood, to talk to Gerald Heard and Huxley. Maybe I'll flatly disagree with them, but I have to hear their case, stated as expertly as possible. And I have to get ready to cope with the war situation, if or when it comes. What are you feeling? What are your plans? You sound so very unperturbed, amidst all the screaming we hear from the distant European shores.

Christopher also showed that in spite of all these new vistas and new preoccupations, he had not forgotten his scout assignment for *New Writing*:

The truth is, we shall never sell New Writing to the U.S.A. on a satisfactory basis until we make it specifically Anglo-American. What we need is to build up a nucleus of really good American writers – such as Steinbeck, Farrell, Caldwell, Hemingway, etc., etc.; so that the Americans can feel that this is ours and their publication. Only then shall we attract the right kind of American proletarian literature, as well. Who is to build up this nucleus? Well, if there isn't a war, and I stay here, I'll do my best. But it will take time.

I sent him a long letter in reply, almost as soon as his arrived, in which I tried to give him an idea of the mood and the way things were going in England, and my own reactions to his new conviction about pacifism. I wrote:

It's odd how people are now beginning to accept a sort of state of 'crisis in permanence', and taking it more calmly, far more calmly, than last autumn. Take our Hogarth Press; we find that orders are out of comparison better than in October-November, and *general* orders, not special orders for a book like BERLIN that's booming (we are well into our fourth thousand now). Not that there hasn't been any jittering. There was far worse, and there still is, but it's somehow more resigned and more hopeful at the same time. You say I sound unperturbed; and really, I believe I have felt extraordinarily quiet ever since January. . . .

I can't convince myself against the argument that the threat of counter-force against force is an essential part of the whole structure of civilization and one's own life – not merely force with guns and tanks but every kind of force. How I wish I could talk it over with you; I want to sympathize and follow what's going on inside, and it's so difficult at this distance. I'm haunted by a song smuggled out of Dachau and written by Jura, the boy who was my Russian teacher in Vienna, who 'died of typhus' early this year without finding freedom again though we had the English visa and everything. I will copy it out and send it to you one of these days. . . .

The Hogarth Press – and literary life in London – and schemes for books and magazines here – form a more and more solid world round me, and I know I've got to go on with it and have made up my mind to see it through longer than another year at the least. . . . I'm terribly pleased that you're going to write that about New York for the next NEW WRITING. I want the MS. just as soon as you can let me have it. And what about all the American stuff you and Wystan promised? Please let me have it as soon as possible. You are absolutely right about N.W. and America, I have always wanted that, and have tried desperately hard. But my American agent hasn't been much use, and I recently realized that it could only be organized from over there. So do your damnedest. Write and tell me all about Hollywood soon.

When Christopher reached Hollywood he dropped the idea of writing a piece about New York, and proposed instead a piece about Ernst Toller whose suicide had deeply affected both him and Wystan. But it never came. The poem by Jura Soyfer I mentioned in my letter was called 'Song of the Austrians in Dachau'. I translated it and published it in *New Writing*. Here is the first verse:

> Pitiless the barbed wire dealing
> Death, that round our prison runs,
> And a sky that knows no feeling
> Sends us ice and burning suns;
> Lost to us the world of laughter,

Lost our homes, our loves, our all;
Through the dawn our thousands muster,
To their work in silence fall.

But the slogan of Dachau is burnt on our brains
And unyielding as steel we shall be;
Are we men, brother? Then we'll be men when they've done,
Work on, we'll go through with the task we've begun,
For work, brother, work makes us free.

Hardly had I got back to England from packing up my life in
Vienna, when the war clouds began to gather more ominously
than ever. Hitler's threats to Poland and our new treaty with that
country made it seem almost impossible for war to be avoided.
Everyone began to prepare. I drew up a memorandum for
Leonard with proposals for the course we should take if the worst
came. 'In the main I agree with all of them,' he wrote from
Rodmell. Essentially, they boiled down to doing nothing in a
hurry, except draw in our horns. I suggested keeping the office
open, though on a restricted basis, and releasing those of the staff
who wanted to join their families or look for war work; going on
with the publication – as far as the changing situation allowed – of
those books we already had in the pipe-line; refusing new books
for at least a month; and getting in as large a supply of paper as
we could (and could afford) before the almost certain rationing
started.

Apart from the possibility of bombing, there was also the
possibility of my being called up into the armed forces sooner or
later (I was thirty-two), or being put to work in one department
or another of the new war bureaucracy – into which a number of
my friends were already beginning to disappear, sucked like ants
into a vast vacuum machine. I had offered my services to the
Foreign Office, where I was foolish enough to believe that my
knowledge of the Danubian countries might prove of some use.
After a long delay, a suggestion was made that I should open a
British bookshop in Bucharest. This exotic plan never got off

the ground, because before even a single book had been ordered, Hitler had overrun Rumania.

When the declaration of war at last came, I was at Fieldhead, but immediately returned to London. I have a vivid recollection of that first week of September. The mornings were hauntingly lovely. Looking out of the window of my first-floor flat, a few doors away from the new Hogarth home in Mecklenburgh Square, I could see the silvery barrage balloons floating high in the sky above the tall plane trees, still and dream-like. Down below in the gardens, one or two soldiers stood on guard by the gun-site in their helmets and khaki greatcoats, also motionless. It was difficult to believe that armies were locked in battle and men dying, far away on the plains of Poland. Everything here was motionless, as if under an enchanter's spell.

The book trade was also motionless, stunned, dead to all appearance. No books were being published, none were being bought in those first few days of war. Nothing stirred behind the sand-bagged shop-fronts of the London bookstores. Everyone expected a pulverizing air-raid, a series of air-raids which would lay the capital in ruins. But none came.

If a deathly stillness seemed to hang over London (though no doubt it was very different within the walls of the Whitehall ministries), all was pandemonium in the country centres to which evacuee children were being sent. On 4 September Leonard wrote to me from Rodmell:

We have been working like coolies here the last 48 hours. Yesterday 18 pregnant women, accompanied each by 3, 4, or 5 already born children arrived in omnibuses. Half an hour later 11 more pregnant women arrived ditto, but with rather fewer already born children. These had to be distributed in inhabited and uninhabited cottages. We spent hours carrying furniture about. On Saturday we expected 100 school children but they got lost on the way and never arrived.

A typical example of Leonard's dry humour. One should remember that Rodmell was only one small village among thousands in the southern counties.

A few days after war was declared the Woolfs came up to town, presumably having stowed the evacuees safely. The move to Mecklenburgh Square had taken place so recently that they had not yet had time to get their new flat on the upper floors of the house into shape. This they proceeded to do; minimum steps at first just to make themselves comfortable, then more boldly during subsequent visits, feeling that to assume the worst would be altogether too demoralizing – though there were plenty of temperamental pessimists about, including Leonard's friend and colleague, Kingsley Martin, editor of the *New Statesman*. They came over to my flat and we all ate sandwiches together, definitely not in the highest spirits. Virginia looked rather distraught, and talked of immersing herself in her diary, though I am inclined to think that more than anything else she was bothered by the slow progress she was making with the biography of Roger Fry, which had become a burden to her. Leonard touched me by saying, quite spontaneously, what bad luck he thought it was for me personally, at the start of a new career in publishing, to have this happen. He talked for some time with the greatest sympathy and understanding, which surprised as well as touched me, in view of the way our relations had been deteriorating and the wrangles that had broken out again during the previous year. It marked the beginning of a period of almost unbroken harmony, which lasted until Virginia's death – and in fact for nearly two years after that catastrophe.

Still the raids did not come. After a few weeks of what came to be called the 'phoney war', Leonard urged me to go out and visit the main provincial towns and discover what the mood was among the booksellers there. Since my return, our travelling had been done by Barbara (Elizabeth) Hepworth, artist and daughter of the famous pioneer film director Cecil Hepworth; a diffident but attractive and intelligent member of the staff. After the first dislocation she decided to stay on, and continued to do some travelling for us. When the Low Countries were invaded, however, she made up her mind to look for war work, not altogether disappointed to leave because she had long felt underpaid and rebellious against Leonard's sudden tyrannical demands in the office, but had held on, like many others, owing to the fascination of the Press and what it was doing.

By the early autumn a little cautious book-buying had started in London. After all, the war had cut off many distractions and pleasures, and in the black-out people had plenty of time to read. Hitler, it seemed, had his hands full in the East for the moment, and the cynical partition of Poland with the Soviet Union was taking place. Perhaps our respite would go on much longer than we had at first thought possible. Perhaps the incredible would happen, and peace of a sort would be made. . . . I found in the provinces that the same cautious hopes were beginning to be entertained. Both Bristol and Bath appeared to have become extensions of the Admiralty: my express down to the West Country was filled with admirals, captains and commanders, covered with gold braid, carrying important-looking briefcases and puffing at their pipes with far-off looks in their sea blue eyes. Bristol not only had its Admiralty offices but the Timber Control as well; the streets were crowded and busy at midday with uniformed bigwigs and bureaucrats hurrying to and from lunch in official cars. The booksellers, certainly not lacking customers with cash to spend in the midst of all this high-powered activity, were already beginning to feel a little more optimistic and were even prepared to prophesy a good Christmas, provided the Nazis didn't start an all-out bombing assault before then. Cambridge, looking its most beautiful in the early autumn sunlight, seemed by comparison almost an hallucination of peace and calm dedication to learning. There, too, the booksellers were recovering from the shock of the outbreak of war, were eager to find out what the Hogarth Press proposed to do, and ready to order books from our small provisional list, and re-order such books as Virginia's works in the bottle-green Uniform Edition. Earlier, Leonard himself had visited two towns within range of his Sussex home, Tunbridge Wells and Reigate, where he considered that the best bookshops in the south-eastern counties were to be found, and reported cautious cheerfulness if not sanguine hopes. The book-sellers liked these personal visits, especially in such difficult times; and that was the way we liked to work.

We took a deep breath, and decided to carry on as normally as possible, with a skeleton staff and what supplies we could get hold of. In the first few weeks manuscripts lay on the shelves, like orphans without prospects, though – to our astonishment – they continued to be offered to us. Then we began to look at them with a reviving interest. Leonard and Virginia decided to make their base at Rodmell, and come up to London for three or four days every two weeks. That routine held all through the winter, during which no call came for me to put on uniform or become a war bureaucrat. We held our regular publishing confabulations in Mecklenburgh Square; but from time to time, as I have already described, I would also go down to Monk's House to spend a night or a couple of nights. Virginia continued to speak wearily of her work on the Roger Fry biography, and Leonard and I urged her, as a counterpoise and refreshment, to get down to the preparation of a third volume – which she had long had in mind –
of her *Common Reader* essays, adding if possible studies of the younger writers she had come to know; she seemed definitely attracted by the idea; but what I certainly did not know, and what even Leonard I believe did not know at that time, was that she had begun work on a new novel – her last, posthumously published, novel *Between the Acts* – which in her diary she writes of under the title she first chose, of *Pointz Hall*. When she at last finished *Roger Fry* in December, her mood was transformed to the most light-hearted gaiety and optimism.

In those early days I wrote again to Christopher, to give him some idea of how things were in the country he had abandoned:

I am writing this in a black-out, and invisible people in tin-helmets are patrolling empty streets, and any moment the warning sirens may start up. I suppose one will get used to that melancholy fading wail, like a dog in unutterable pain, but it gave me a funny feeling in the pit of

Julian Bell in 1930

The Bells' garden at Charleston
in the 1930s

The author with Virginia Woolf at Monk's House, Rodmell, 1931

Tavistock Square in 1904: the south side

Stephen Spender in 1932

Christopher Isherwood in 1936

The author

Leonard at Monk's House, 1938

Virginia at Monk's House, 1938

The garden at Monk's House, 1938

Leonard, Virginia and Sally. Rodmell, 1938

Some Hogarth Press jacket designs: *Party Going* and *A Letter to a Young Poet*
designed by John Banting; *Goodbye to Berlin* designed by Hans Wild; and the
1939 Catalogue designed by Vanessa Bell

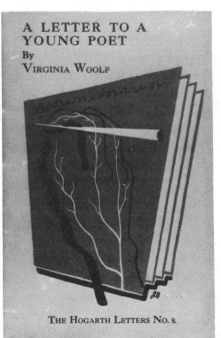

The author, in his Home Guard uniform, prepares to meet the enemy

The author and Leonard Woolf at work in the author's flat in Carrington House, 1944

my stomach when I first heard it through my half-dreams. It's the oddest kind of war up to date, nobody excited, only bitter and depressed and grim, and no sign of hysteria against the Germans as Germans yet. But how long will that last against frayed nerves, and noise, and casualties? I suppose one will get used to all sorts of things sooner or later. Life has changed so much and so fast already, like one picture fading into another in a film. And even if the war only lasts a few months, I don't suppose it will ever be the same again. . . .

Christopher wrote back from Santa Monica before the end of September:

All my thoughts are with you. How much simpler things wd. have been if it had come in September [1938], and we'd shared the flat. Since then, I've made a lot of rash decisions, and God knows where they will eventually land me. To Berthold and myself, you in England are all partly sacred – not to be laughed at or even smiled over – like the blessed martyrs. No doubt the atmosphere on the spot is altogether less rarified – but such are the reactions of neutrals.

I had said in my letter that we hoped to 'find some lean war substitute for *New Writing*' – the third number of the New Series had come out within a few weeks of the declaration. I had already laid plans for this change by the time his answer arrived. The chief trouble of the Hogarth Press during the war was finding paper; a difficulty severely aggravated by the extreme smallness of its quota as soon as rationing began to be strictly applied. As I have already mentioned, we bought up a certain amount of paper at the outbreak of war (not much because we didn't dare take too big a risk), but by the middle of 1940 there was scarcely any of that left. Unfortunately, in the twelve months that were chosen as a yardstick by the Paper Control we had ordered comparatively little; and when it came to being allowed only forty per cent of that we were reduced to something well under ten tons a year. In fact, I believe it was nearer five tons. Now this will probably mean very little indeed to those who have never had anything to do with book production. I will therefore take an example, though jumping ahead a little, which I hope will give a rough idea of the problems we faced, without going into complicated details.

I find a note among my files about the paper we consumed during the year beginning 1 March 1942. During that year we published Virginia's *Death of the Moth*, a collection of essays to take the place of the projected but never prepared third *Common Reader*. It had been put together by Leonard after Virginia's death, but of course he could only guess at the selection Virginia would have made from the great mass of essays and review articles which had never been assembled into book form. It was a demy octavo volume of 160 closely printed pages, with the obligatory note at the beginning 'printed in complete conformity with the authorized economy standards'. We reprinted it almost immediately after publication, and again before the year's end. These three editions, or rather impressions, consumed just over 50 cwt of paper, that is $2\frac{1}{2}$ tons. If you take our total annual ration as $6\frac{1}{2}$ tons, you can see what an inroad this one (of course exceptional) book made in it. In the same year we also needed reprints of other works by Virginia, which took up another 2 tons. In addition, we had to reprint more than one of our psycho-analytical books. The result was that there was really hardly anything left for other new books. I must, however, add that the Paper Control maintained a special reserve of paper from which extra allocations of paper could be made for books of medical and educational value, or of special value for the war effort – which included important export orders. The details are lost, but I am under the impression that some of the psycho-analytical books benefited from this concession. Even so, the situation was almost desperate for us all the time, until rationing was relaxed. Unlike the big publishing houses with a comparatively ample quota we had scarcely any room for manoeuvre at all, especially if more than one of our books became a best-seller. There was also the problem, which we had to envisage, of providing paper for un-expected new books by our most successful authors, or losing them to publishing houses which could accommodate them much more easily within their larger quotas.

After the Paternoster Row disaster at the end of December 1940 (to which I shall come back shortly) *all* books sold well; but of course there was a large difference between a good sale of one of Virginia's books, for instance, and a good sale of a book of poetry. When the shoe began to pinch especially hard, sometime between 1942 and 1943, a group of about a dozen small book publishers, that is publishers with an annual allocation (at 40 per cent) of less than 20 tons each, banded together to press the urgency of their case on the Ministry of Supply. We pointed out how unfairly the system worked as between small publishers and the big houses such as Methuen or Macmillan; we asked for our quota to be raised from 40 per cent to 100 per cent; and we reminded the Ministry what a drop in the ocean of the total supplies of paper to publishers this would mean. We kept a close eye on developments in the United States, where paper control had also been introduced soon after their entry into the war at the end of 1941, and were heartened to find that the Bookpublishers' Bureau in that country were well aware of the problems which faced the small American book publishers; we had reason to believe that the authorities were ready to establish an all-round minimum quota to relieve their plight. Above all we pointed out how disproportionate a contribution small publishers had made to the arts and education. Nevertheless one cannot look back with anything but amazement on the fact that – such was the obstruction of the war bureaucracy in Britain, in spite of the sympathy we found among several influential politicians, and though the general quota had been raised twice by very small percentages as the supply position eased – the war was actually over before our plea for 100 per cent was granted.

In any case, in 1939 Leonard and I had to think very hard about our publishing strategy. We soon agreed that the first priority was Virginia's work, both in bringing out new books and in keeping the earlier books in print. We had brought out

Freud's *Moses and Monotheism* in the spring with considerable success; we decided that all his works were our next priority, and indeed all the other volumes in the International Psycho-Analytical Library must be kept in print as far as possible: to lose any of them, let alone all of them, would be a major financial set-back for the Press, quite apart from their importance as works of learning and research. Again, if Leonard himself were to write new books (his play *The Hotel* came out in 1939, and his *Barbarians at the Gate* had been a Left Book Club choice in the same year), they must also have a high priority: I interpreted that as part of the bargain when I became a 50 per cent partner. Leonard himself, after his first angry challenge at the beginning of 1939, no longer questioned that my book-magazine *New Writing* should continue to be published twice a year as before, if conditions allowed. The 'lean war substitute' I had worked out was *Folios of New Writing*, 160 pages of many fewer words than the 284 pages, with illustrations, of the New Series No. 3. We also had obligations to our recently recruited author, Henry Green, who produced new books in 1940 (*Pack My Bag*), 1943 (*Caught*), and 1945 (*Loving*) before the war was over. Luckily (but only in this sense) Christopher Isherwood produced nothing for us after *Goodbye to Berlin*. We had taken on Tom Hopkinson, as I have described, soon after I arrived back at the Press, but his next novel to follow *The Man Below*, *Mist on the Tagus*, was not ready till late in 1945.

These priorities left very little indeed for any other kind of publishing, though in 1940 we brought out Stephen Spender's novel *The Backward Son*, which we hoped would be followed by other fiction; and a little later we persuaded Raymond Mortimer to make a selection from the admirable critical articles and reviews he had written over many years, and published it as *Channel Packet*. In addition, in 1943 we took on the new, brilliantly gifted author William Sansom. What I felt very keenly was that the Press should somehow or other keep the flag of poetry flying – a flag that had been one of its chief distinctions before the war, especi-

ally in the series of the Hogarth Living Poets. If we kept that flag
flying, young authors would know that we were still interested
in them. Since my return to the Press in 1938, I had started a series
called 'Poets of Tomorrow', one of the chief aims of which, in
my eyes, was to show that we could produce poetry as elegantly
as any other publisher, and not merely in the rather mean,
reach-me-down get-up of the Living Poets. I had secured enough
rather good, attractive paper for three volumes, and so it was
possible to publish a second selection (which was *Cambridge
Poetry 1940* and included for the first time poems by Terence
Tiller), and a third selection (which had eight of David Gascoyne's
most beautiful wartime poems) even in 1942; but obviously now
something rather different from these anthologies, and less
extravagantly produced, was called for. In the 1914–18 war poetry
had been very much in demand; why not then take the fairly easy
gamble that the same demand would occur in this war? The
Woolfs were pleased with the idea: it would keep up our name
for avant-garde publishing at very little cost in paper consumption,
and we all thought it would be fun to do. So it was that the New
Hogarth Library was born. During the course of the war we
published fourteen volumes, containing fifty or sixty pages each:
it was in my opinion a very fine list, which only one other
publisher in London could rival – Faber & Faber with T. S. Eliot
as poetry editor. We started off with selections from Cecil Day
Lewis and William Plomer, both of whom had originally been
Hogarth authors, and then went on to three notable translations:
the Spender-Gili versions from Lorca, Norman Cameron's from
Rimbaud (in fact a first publication), and a selection from the
many translations from Rilke J. B. Leishman had done for the
Press over the years. Finding success and popularity for the series,
we went on to original volumes of work by living poets: first
books by Laurie Lee (*The Sun My Monument*) and Terence Tiller
(*Poems*, followed by *The Inward Animal* as I shall later relate), two
books (*A Lost Season* and *The Middle of a War*) by Roy Fuller,
who became one of the half-dozen really outstanding English

war poets; and an unusual mixed volume of new poetry, *Work in Hand*, by Robert Graves and two of his close younger associates at that time, Norman Cameron and Alan Hodge. A small enough venture in all conscience, but I think the poetic vitamin content was high, and the volumes as they came out were eagerly snapped up, not least by the more intelligent young men who were serving in the armed forces.

By Christmas 1939 publishing in Britain could almost be described as flourishing, in spite of the fact that the big publishing houses were losing more and more of their staff to the call-up. If this early phase still ranked as the 'phoney' war in people's minds, it was of course an illusion, for at sea the Royal Navy was engaged in ceaseless offensive and defensive activities.

Then, in the spring of 1940, the illusion was at last smashed, and Hitler began his drive to the West. The series of devastating shocks followed one another without respite: Holland, Belgium, Norway fallen; France invaded, and the British Army just escaping from Dunkirk, but with all its armour lost. Psychologically the worst blow was the fall of Paris. Leonard took this very hard; and I remember the evening before Reynaud's speech, when Tom Eliot and William Plomer and I were dining with them, he suddenly fell very silent, looking utterly overwhelmed, and we had to break off our discussion about the French collapse, for fear he should collapse himself. The realization that the full might of Nazi Germany faced us directly across the Channel was grim indeed; and yet, with a new government headed by Churchill in power, the effect, in the midst of dismay, was curiously exhilarating. We braced ourselves for invasion, without believing it quite possible . . . after nine hundred years? A rather absurd spy mania broke out, and a few days after the fall of Paris Leonard, his poise recovered, produced a wonderful story of how, on a train journey to London, Virginia had insisted in a stage whisper that a perfectly innocent nun who got into their carriage was a Nazi paratrooper in disguise. In August the expected air war over southern England began in earnest; but it was not until the beginning of September that the major Luftwaffe attacks on London were launched.

I happened to be down in Wiltshire, near Salisbury, staying with my sister Helen and her soldier husband who was waiting for a posting, on the evening of 7 September. Alarm calls suddenly came through after dinner for my brother-in-law from local Army headquarters. An invasion, it was hinted, might be launched at any moment, and he had to change as fast as he could into his battledress and dash off into the night. As everyone knows, no attempt at invasion in fact took place; but we heard at midnight that gigantic air-raids on London had begun. I had at all costs to try and get back the next afternoon, and picturing central London as a smoking ruin it seemed to me extremely unlikely that I should succeed. My train from Salisbury started on time, but on the outskirts of London, about 5.30 pm, we ran into trouble. A major air battle was taking place overhead in the cloudless blue sky, with sudden whining zooms and the intermittent rattle of machine-gun fire clearly audible. The train crept on by fits and starts, finding the signals against it almost every half mile. Time dragged on, light began to fade, and an atmosphere of increasingly tense anxiety pervaded the train. Soldiers – their leave-passes running out – began to jump off and slip through the back gardens of houses by the track to find a main road and buses. Civilians grabbed their hand-luggage and joined them, and I followed too, the ludicrous expostulations of the elderly guard in my ears: 'Never known passengers behave like this before in all my forty years on the line. . . . Quite against the regulations. . . . I don't know, I don't know what we're coming to . . . etc., etc.' Luckily I found a bus bound for the West End almost at once, and in spite of the sirens that sounded again within a few minutes, the driver charged recklessly on through the now moonlit deserted streets. When I eventually jumped off, I could see the glow of fires started by the bombs all through Holborn, but I managed to reach my as yet undamaged flat in Mecklenburgh Square, swallowed a quick snack for my dinner, and lay down on my bed to await events.

Very soon a new air-raid began. I could hear bombs falling and gunfire in the distance. The clatter grew nearer; then suddenly there were three loud, whistling, tearing noises close overhead, and each time violent concussions were followed by the sound of tinkling glass. . . . I shall not go into the details of that night of explosions and fires, smashed windows and flying masonry, but before it was over the Air Raid Wardens judged the houses on our side of the Square to be unsafe, and instructed us to go to the nearest basement shelter as fast as we could. When dawn at last came, we found that there was an unexploded time-bomb in the garden, almost directly opposite the Hogarth Press, and the whole Square was being cordoned off and evacuated.

When I managed to get back a few days later, the time-bomb had gone off, causing havoc to No. 37. All the windows had gone, and part of the ceiling of the basement front room had crashed down, covering everything with dust and lumps of plaster and splinters of wood. Not long afterwards, a land-mine fell at the back of the house, blasting all the rooms that had escaped the damage caused by the time-bomb. As Leonard has described it, 'books, files, paper, the printing machine and the cases of type were in a horrible grimy mess. The roof had been so badly damaged that in several places it let the rain in, and the water-pipes in the house had been so badly shaken by the blast that occasionally one burst without warning and sent a waterfall down the stairs from the third floor to the ground floor.' As a result of these inundations, and possibly the hoses of the firemen as well, masses of letters and precious documents were reduced to sodden pulp and lost for ever.

A week or two after the land-mine had fallen, I made my way again to wrecked Mecklenburgh Square, managed to get into No. 37, and found Leonard and Virginia upstairs, picking about among the ruins of their flat. Rubble and broken glass were everywhere; and yet I was surprised to see that most of the books were in their shelves and the pictures bright and straight on the walls – perhaps the first task they had undertaken. They both seemed remarkably cheerful in spite of the desolation of their home that surrounded them. Leonard remarked, grinning at me, 'Well, really, possessions are such a nuisance, perhaps it will be a good thing to start clear again.'

In any case No. 37 was now uninhabitable, and unlikely we thought to be mended before the end of the war. So was my own flat: the house had a cross chalked on the door, reminding me grimly of accounts of the Plague Year. An emergency scheme for the continued existence of the Press had to be decided upon at once. We had a brainwave. A large proportion of our books were being printed at that time by a small firm called the Garden City Press at Letchworth, about an hour in the train north-east of London in the direction of Cambridge. It occurred to us that they might be ready to help, as they were extremely anxious to keep our custom. We approached them, and they immediately said they would find accommodation for us if we just brought the essential files and ledgers down with us. They offered us two rooms at the top of the printing works, where at least I and two others could work. It was not particularly convenient to have to make regular weekly journeys down to Letchworth, but the plan had the enormous advantage, in those days of constantly interrupted communications, of putting the actual production of our books under the same roof as our own publishing work. With very little initial trouble, it worked extremely well, and the Hogarth Press was lodged there until the end of the war. I took a small furnished apartment in London, and an even smaller one in Cambridge, as wild horses – or rather wild Nazis – would not have dragged me to spend any nights in the smug suburbia of Letchworth. My general routine was to leave the family home at Bourne End on Monday morning, spend a night in London, then on to Letchworth where I worked in the middle of the week, but continued by train to my room in Cambridge every night. On Thursday or Friday evening I would return to London, and spend the weekend either at Fieldhead again or with Leonard and Virginia in Sussex. This may sound complicated, but in fact it proved simple, though during that horrible winter of 1940–41 the trains from Letchworth to London after dark were constantly – on fine nights – being brought to a halt by air-raids. I can remember few things more unpleasant in the war than waiting cooped up in a train without lights outside a station, while Goering's bombers were chased by the searchlights and the ack-ack guns through the night skies. My then secretary, Michael Nelson, was often with me on these journeys before he was called up, and we used to cheer one another during the ominous stops by telling (or inventing) crazy stories about our mutual friends.

I have already hinted at the disaster of crucial significance for the book-trade that took place at the end of December. During a particularly heavy raid on London, Paternoster Row in the City, very close to St Paul's Cathedral, was destroyed by incendiary bombs. Paternoster Row happened to be the place where a large number of publishers warehoused a great proportion of their stock of books. When morning came, these hundreds of thousands of books had been consumed by the flames. The result was that an extreme dearth of books began to be felt very soon after, and became more and more evident as the months went by. The demand for something, anything, to read was increasing at the same time. Those publishers – and the Hogarth Press was one of them – who were lucky enough not to have been affected, or only slightly, by the conflagration, began to sell their stocks at a gallop. Books that in peacetime, when there was an abundance of choice, would have sold only a few copies every month, were snapped up the moment they arrived in the shops. It may seem a paradox that the Hogarth Press, for instance, steadily increased its turnover while its production of new books decreased; but the disease of all modern book publishing in Britain – and in other Western countries I think as well – too many books chasing too few customers, had been cured for the time being by Dr Hitler's rather drastic remedies.

Once the Hogarth Press had been evacuated to Letchworth, we were able to pursue our publishing programme, within the limitations of our paper ration, with quiet diligence. After the destruction of their house the Woolfs remained at Rodmell, Leonard, sometimes accompanied by Virginia, only coming up to London from time to time, generally for the day. This meant that almost the whole responsibility for running the Press fell on my shoulders. I sent detailed, almost daily, reports to Leonard, but it was only natural that he should sometimes feel that he was kept in the dark, particularly as posts did not always work very promptly and packets were delayed – sometimes lost – in spite of my strict instructions to the staff about not missing the collections. This caused occasional friction between Letchworth and Rodmell, but such troubles were, at the beginning at least, quickly put right.

During the period between September 1940 and the end of the London blitz in May 1941, therefore, as the Garden City Press was never hit we were lucky in having no major interruptions to cope with. This was not the fortune of many other publishers, who would wake one morning to hear that the printing works outside London where a number of their important books were being produced had been victims of the Luftwaffe, roofs blown off, plant smashed and printed sheets waiting for delivery to the binders set on fire. Such alarms and excursions often meant long delays, for one thing because the printers, like the publishers, were working with reduced staffs as the call-up thinned their ranks.

If I did not experience these crises as Managing Partner of the Hogarth Press, I knew them all too well under my other hat, as editor of *Penguin New Writing*. My bi-annual book-magazine had, during the autumn of 1940, given birth to a vigorous foal in the stable of Allen Lane and his Penguin Books. The first two numbers of *Penguin New Writing* were intended as a cheap paper-back anthology of some of the best contributions that had appeared in the hard-back volumes, but such was the success of No. 1 that Allen Lane readily agreed to my suggestion to turn it into a magazine intended to appear monthly, with part of the contents still consisting of anthology selections as before, but part entirely new material – as it turned out, largely from the younger writers who were being absorbed into the armed forces. It became astonishingly popular: Allen Lane soon gave it a print order of 75, 000 copies, but at its peak even that large circulation was exceeded. The snag, however, lay in the increasing difficulties of the printers I have just described; those, and Allen Lane's problem of allocating his paper ration among the many titles on his flourishing list, soon made the idea of monthly publication a chimaera pursued with ever remoter success. I fretted and fought; but the sleepless, careworn faces of the works managers when I travelled down to correct proofs, soon convinced my impatient self that patience had to be learned.

I have described how Virginia's mood was transformed when she finished her biography of Roger Fry in December 1940; and though Leonard had, unusually, found rather severe fault with it, his criticism was countered in her mind by Vanessa's and Margery Fry's warm admiration. As the moment for publication approached, however, in the middle of the Battle of Britain, her ineluctable anxieties began to prey on her again. I had read a proof, but I was so busy at the time that I did not write to her immediately, as I would have if it had been a novel. This troubled her (as her diary reveals), though she did not reveal her disappointment except indirectly in the letter she wrote me at the end of July. I had asked her if I might print her 'Leaning Tower' address to the Brighton branch of the Workers' Educational Association in *Folios of New Writing*:

I'm quite pleased with the sales of R.F. so far – L. is binding more. Don't bother to read it now, but some day I should value your opinion very much. It's no good reading other people's books when one's writing one's own. I hope your Penguin is a fully feathered bird by this time, with a vast throat to swallow all the sprats.

I'd like you to print the Leaning Tower, if I can bring myself to revise it, which I loathe. Also, when would you want it – also, what about America? I mean can I print it simultaneously there? But at the moment I can't stop reading Coleridge – thanks to you I'm lured back into the ancients, and read a William Morris, Chants for Socialists, with immense pleasure. So I can't bring myself to do anything I ought to do.

If I had failed myself to read *Roger Fry*, my mother had, and at once wrote a letter of appreciation to Virginia. She answered on 25 July:

Dear Mrs Lehmann, your letter gave me so much pleasure that I must answer it in spite of the fact that you forbid me. I was so afraid that I hadn't been able to convey anything of Roger Fry, that it is a great relief to me to find that you, who didn't know him, feel his great charm. I only hope that there will be more readers like you – anyhow, its a great comfort to have one. I never found a piece of work so difficult.

Its a bad time to bring a book out, and I'm specially sorry on John's account. Its been so hard on him, beginning his work with the war. All the same, both Leonard and I feel that the partnership is turning out a great success, at any rate from our point of view. Its years since Leonard has had such a free time. And I'm sure, when the war ends, John will make a great success of it.

All during the summer that part of Sussex where Rodmell lies was in the direct line of the battle taking place in the air. Virginia's mood was strangely euphoric: it was almost as if she relished being under the threat of external danger which took her mind off the danger which threatened her from within. In fact, I have always been convinced that she didn't take her own life because of despair caused by the terrors of the war. It is true that Leonard, as a Jew and a socialist, knew that he would have short shrift if the Nazis invaded and occupied at least the southern part of England. It is true that he and Virginia had made up their minds that if the worst came to the worst they would commit suicide together. But by the time the concentrated bombardment of London began the danger of invasion, at least for that year, had faded. Again, I always found that Leonard had a reasoned optimism about the outcome of the war, and in many talks with me he had made it clear that he was very far from sharing the defeatism that from time to time overcame some of his colleagues even when things looked particularly black. Nor was Virginia herself of nervous or pessimistic temperament in practical life; in fact she was a very cool and courageous person. After her death I remembered how, during the time when British and Nazi fighters were battling day after day in the air above Rodmell, she wrote me a very cheerful and amusing letter about the diversions they could have produced for me if I came down to stay with them at Monk's House. 'We could have offered you,' she wrote, 'a great variety of air-raid alarms, distant bombs, reports by Mrs Bleach who brought a stirrup pump (installed, needless to say, in my bedroom) of battles out at sea. Indeed its rather lovely about 2 in the morning to see the lights stalking the Germans over the marshes. But this remains on tap, so you must propose yourself later.'

And I also remembered how, not long after their London house had been bombed, I had met her wandering along Guildford Street with Leonard one afternoon, both a little confused in the midst of the air-raid that was taking place, but Virginia very smiling and collected – more so in fact than Leonard. We found a vantage point from which we could view the damage that had been done to Mecklenburgh Square; and after a few minutes the only gesture she allowed herself was to touch Leonard's arm and say quietly: 'Leo, there are aeroplanes overhead, don't you think we ought to take cover?'

All through the writing of *Pointz Hall* her diary reveals her as being extraordinarily buoyant and happy about her work, As late as 23 November, when she had finished it first time over, she could write: 'I am a little triumphant about the book. I think its an interesting attempt in a new method. I think its more quintessential than the others. More milk skimmed off. A richer pat, certainly a fresher than that misery *The Years*. I've enjoyed writing almost every page.' But there was still a good deal of rewriting and rearranging to be done, as anyone who has studied the various drafts in the New York Public Library can testify, and it was not until the last days of February 1941 that she finally completed her revisions, changed the name to *Between the Acts*, and showed it to Leonard.

One day, about a fortnight later, they both came up to London for one of our regular, but by then rarer, meetings. We met for lunch at St Stephen's Tavern. I have described the episode in detail in my autobiography; and quote it now as it comes almost in its entirety from the diary notes I made at the time:

We had a table by the window on the first floor, looking out on Parliament Square and Big Ben, and I can clearly remember how brilliant the spring sunshine was in which the whole scene was steeped.

The week before, I had sent them Terence Tiller's first book of poems, with a strong recommendation that we should publish it. They had brought it with them: Virginia liked it, and declared that in her opinion the Press should accept it. Leonard grumbled about the obscurity of the young poets, and taking a sheet here and there out of the folder, challenged me: 'But parse this poem, John, *parse* it!' Virginia came to my rescue, maintaining that he was being too logical, that there was music and imagination in the poetry that was rare for a first book. Leonard's objections, however, were only a rear-guard feint, and I soon saw that he had made up his mind to yield to our majority opinion – that in fact he agreed with us more than he had been prepared to admit at first. This was the last book Virginia was to read and approve for the Press.

During our argument I noticed that she seemed in a state of unusual nervous tension, her hand shaking slightly now and then. I began to feel that there was some awkward subject they wanted to bring up. I had been aware for some time that Virginia was at work on a new book, but I had no inkling what it was, and knew her well enough not to press for details she was clearly reluctant to give. Then Leonard revealed the secret: she had written a new novel, which had been given the tentative title of *Between the Acts*. This was exciting news for the Press as well as for me as a devotee of her work, but when I turned to congratulate her she began to talk about the book in great agitation, trying to damp down my enthusiasm and saying that it was no good at all and obviously couldn't be published. Leonard rebuked her gently, telling her that she ought to know that it was one of the best things she had written. They went on arguing for some time, Leonard trying to calm her with the firmness of his conviction, until I pleaded to be allowed to read it and give my opinion. I could not believe that under any circumstance a new novel by Virginia could be 'no good'. Finally she agreed to think it over when she got back to Rodmell, and let me see the typescript if she was in any doubt.

Before we left, she suddenly said she had nothing to do now, and could I send her some reading. I told her I would gladly pick out some manuscripts from the latest batch that had arrived for *Folios of New Writing*, if she really meant it. She eagerly agreed. Looking back on that request afterwards, when the tragedy was over, I realized that her need to have something to occupy and steady her mind was desperate.

A few days later a letter arrived from her, dated 20 March:

Dear John: I've just read my so-called novel over: and I really don't think it does. Its much too slight and sketchy. Leonard doesn't agree. So we've decided to ask you if you'd mind reading it and give your casting vote? Meanwhile, don't take any steps.

I'm sorry to trouble you, but I feel fairly certain it would be a mistake from all points of view to publish it. But as we both differ about this, your opinion would be a great help.

She added a postscript, saying that she hoped I would send her the manuscripts for her to read, which I had in fact already done. But this letter caused me some embarrassment as well as eager anticipation. I was so used to her self-disparagement when she had a new work ready, and felt so certain that we should in the end publish the book, that I had added an advance announcement of it to an advertisement I had just prepared, in some hurry, for the Spring Books number of the *New Statesman*. I wrote back to her at once:

Dear Virginia: A little alarmed at your note, because following our lunch together, and Leonard's very definite suggestion, I announced your book to the New Statesman and have gone into their literary number with it. L. was very keen about this, and indeed it would have been a great mistake not to announce everything we could, as they won't have another Spring number. You will, I hope, forgive me about this: I felt quite certain from our talk that the question of publication had already been decided – and it is now too late to reverse the wheels. All the same I will not let this influence my opinion about the book. So do please send it to me as soon as possible – to Fieldhead. I can't say how much I look forward to reading it, and giving a casting vote. I will take no more steps meanwhile.

The typescript was already on its way to me. I was due to go out on Home Guard duty the evening it arrived, but I plunged into it at once, and finished it before I went off into the night with my rifle and tin hat. It was a thrilling experience, and I was deeply moved. It seemed to me to have an unparalleled imaginative power, to be filled with a poetry more disturbing than anything she had written before, reaching at times the extreme limits of the communicable. This effect was curiously heightened by the eccentric typing – Virginia's typing was always eccentric and sometimes her spelling too – but on this occasion it gave an extraordinary impression, as if a high-voltage electric current had been running through her fingers. I sent an urgent message to Rodmell the next morning, announcing that as far as I was concerned there was no question at all: my casting vote was unequivocally for publication.

Her reply came at the weekend. It wasn't at all what I had hoped; and it was enclosed in a letter from Leonard that shocked and dismayed me, in spite of the warning signs I had noticed at our lunch in London: he had had no chance to tell me of the crisis they had already been through, which he has described so poignantly in his autobiography. He now warned me that Virginia was on the verge of a complete nervous breakdown; she was so seriously ill that she could not possible revise the book as she suggested, and we must therefore put it off indefinitely. He asked me to send the typescript back to her, with a letter to say how sorry we were that we could not publish it in the spring, but would hope for the autumn. He added that she had never-theless been very pleased with my letter about it. This was the letter he enclosed:

Dear John, I'd decided, before your letter came, that I can't publish that novel as it stands – its too silly and trivial. What I will do is to revise it, and see if I can pull it together and so publish it in the autumn. If published as it is, it would certainly mean a financial loss; which we don't want. I am sure I am right about this.

I needn't say how sorry I am to have troubled you. The fact is it was written in the intervals of doing Roger with my brain half asleep. I didn't realise how bad it was till I read it over. Please forgive me, and believe I'm only doing what is best.

I'm sending back the MSS with my notes.

Again I apologize profoundly.

By the time this letter reached me it was all over. On the Monday I had another letter from Leonard, breaking the incredible news that she had drowned herself. Though he ran down to the river the moment he found her farewell note, he was too late to prevent her. All he could find was her walking stick lying on the river bank. Just after she disappeared, the tide had turned and poured out to sea. Her body was not found for several weeks.

In the last letter he wrote to me about it, Leonard said, apropos *Between the Acts*:

She was very pleased when she got your letter about it. I still think it a very remarkable book. I had expected from what she said and feared to find a loss of vigour. I may be wrong, but it seemed to me the opposite, to be more vigorous and pulled together than most of her other books, to have more depth and to be very moving. I also thought that the strange symbolism gave it an almost terrifying profundity and beauty.

He decided to publish it just as it was, with only the spelling and other minor textual confusions put right and instructions to the printer added. In this I entirely concurred with him. She had said, before it was published, that even *To the Lighthouse* was 'inconceivably bad'; and in those last days she was so ill that in any case she was no fit judge of whether it was 'too silly and trivial'. Nor was she telling the truth when she said that it was written 'in the intervals of doing Roger with my brain half asleep'. On the contrary, the frequent entries in her diary prove that *Roger Fry* became a wearisome grind, and *Between the Acts* always a refreshing holiday from it. In one point, however, I disagree with Leonard. In the Note he put in the front of the published version, he maintained that 'She would not have made any large or material alterations in it, though she would probably have made a good many small corrections or revisions before passing the final proofs.' It is a risky assumption, because we know – and Leonard knew as well as anyone – that when she revised she always did a great deal more than make 'small corrections or revisions', even cutting out whole paragraphs and adding vital new material right down to the last proof. I have always thought it possible that in a final revision she might have integrated some of the scenes of the Pageant – the pastiche of Restoration comedy, for instance – more completely into the total design of the book. Be that as it may, what struck me at the first reading, and what strikes me again every time I reread it, apart from the profound visionary insight of so many passages, is that Virginia had recovered her strong sense of form, which, if we had nothing to go by after *The Years*, we might well feel she was in danger of losing.

About two weeks later Leonard returned to London, and we had lunch together at my Club. I was moved by his fortitude in discussing everything that had happened, and the changes Virginia's death were likely to make in his own life and our future as publishers, though it was perfectly clear to me, from the moment I saw him, how deeply he had suffered. He told me then that he believed she had made a first attempt about a week before, because one day he had met her in the garden coming back from a walk, all trembling and dripping with water. I think he blamed himself for not having been more alert after that warning; but it is difficult to see what more he could have done than he was already doing – except to take the dangerous step of insisting on her having a nurse in constant attendance.

It relieved me, for his sake and for my own sake too, to hear him speak of the future with cool decision: everything was to go on as far as possible as before, he looked to me to manage the affairs of the Press from London and Letchworth (always keeping him in close touch of course), while he went on working mainly at Rodmell. He already saw that there would be an enormous amount of work for him to do as Virginia's literary executor. As I had known since my early days at the Press, she had scarcely ever stopped writing: when it was not a long work it was essays or articles or short stories, and in addition to all the periodical work (so much of it written anonymously) and all the manuscripts left in a finished or half-finished state in her desk, there were the many volumes of her diary and her voluminous correspondence neither of which Leonard, except for the extremely curtailed *Writer's Diary*, ever reached. We talked a little about her illness, and I found that he confirmed the more or less complete conviction that I had come to myself, that the fundamental cause of the breakdown had not been the war, but the strain she had put the delicate mechanism of her mind and imagination under in bringing her new novel to a conclusion, a strain that had so nearly brought a return of madness when she was finishing *The Waves* and *The Years*. This time she had not believed she could avoid it, as her farewell letter, which Leonard told me about but did not show me, made clear.

Her body had not yet been found when Leonard and I had that meeting. Perhaps he hoped it never would be found, and he never would have to identify it; but he was not spared even that final ordeal.

When Leonard gave me a general picture of the posthumous volumes of her work that he would make it his business to bring out, a programme that would obviously extend over a long period of years – though I don't think even he at that time realized how long – I had a curious feeling of solace, as if Virginia the writer was still to be with us; but the prospect was nevertheless only a small consolation for the absence of Virginia in person from the activities of the Press. Apart from my grief at her death as the loss of a worshipped friend, I was oppressed with melancholy at the thought that she, who had seemed at least as essential a part of the spirit of the Press as Leonard, and whose retirement from partnership when I took over had been little more than a technical formality, would no longer be there to discuss the manuscripts that came in, to gossip about the authors if they were already known or to speculate with free fantasy about them if they were not, to plan new anthologies and new series with us, and to laugh over the day-to-day alarms and excursions in our office life. I was to find even greater cause for regretting her absence a few years later.

I wanted to write a poem about her then; but I couldn't bring myself to do more than write a prose elegy, a kind of funeral oration, which was published in the French magazine *Fontaine*, founded in Algeria as soon as the Allied armies had cleared North Africa of the Germans and Italians. It was only three decades later, at a time when I was studying her work again intensively in order to write a book about her, that the words came at last. I called it 'The Lady of Elvedon', writing it round the famous visionary experience that Bernard and Susan have in an early section of *The Waves*:

> The waves close over us, and the green air
> Of beech leaves meets above our heads:
> We are the first explorers crouching here
> To learn what the walled garden hides.
>
> Hush: the red funguses and ferns smell strong,
> Primeval fir cones fall to rot
> Among the grasses; sleeping daws take wing;
> And someone, see, will stay to write,

Ransomed as in eternity, between
The two long windows that face the lawn
The gardeners sweep for ever; she has won
The game with death and keeps the crown.

The stable clock stands still, and tells no hour:
Virginia, it is you I see,
The Lady of Elvedon in that timeless air
That knows of no mortality.

And you become your image of the art
You kept such faith with, that the frail
Structure of tissue and nerve sustained a hurt
Only the final peace could heal.

And as I read that passage I recall
You in your studio, where each day
Whether sun blest outside or the rain fell,
So sure of what mere words could do

To make the shape of loveliness and truth
Clear as a pool in evening light
Before the voices of pursuing wrath
Mocked you with sentence of Too Late,

Your hand moved like the Lady of Elvedon's hand
Still writing – was it poem or prose? –
Until the Lighthouse gained at last, you found
Your vision. We are left to praise.

PART IV

LEONARD WITHOUT VIRGINIA

IN the spring of 1939 Christopher had written to me, in a letter I have already quoted, that if war did not break out he wanted to help turn *New Writing*, as we had always wanted, into a truly Anglo-American literary magazine, and collect American contributors 'so that the Americans can feel that it is ours and their publication'. But war *had* broken out, and Christopher was deeply involved in the spiritual self-examination that was to change him into a pacifist and a follower of Vedanta. All that he was able to do was to urge me to be on the look-out for the work of Peter Viertel, the young son of Berthold. I published a good story of his, 'Smudge', in the second number of *Folios of New Writing*, but was unable to take on his first novel which had just appeared in New York. Later, he persuaded Lincoln Kirstein to send me his book *For My Brother*, 'a true story by Jose Martinez Berlanga as told to Lincoln Kirstein'. It seemed to me a most unusual and moving book, and I was very happy to publish it in 1943. 'Lincoln must have written in a kind of mediumistic state,' Christopher wrote. 'I really flatter myself that you would never have seen it if I hadn't literally nagged him about it every single time I wrote or saw him.'

Christopher and I continued to write to one another all during the war, but after *For My Brother* his part in this story of my relations with the Woolfs and the Hogarth Press came to an end. When he next produced a work of fiction, *Prater Violet*, it was published by Methuen, so fulfilling the contract he had signed with them after the publication of *Mr Norris* for his future full-length works of fiction; a move to which he had been persuaded, according to his own story, by the lack of any special interest shown him by the Woolfs after my first departure. And when he visited England again after the war, I had already broken with the Press.

The story had a sad, symbolic postscript. I quote from my diary, summer of 1941:

Today I fulfilled a long-standing promise, and went down to 19 Pembroke Gardens to see Christopher's mother about his books. A rainy, dark-green July afternoon. The house looked incredibly desolate inside, bare floors, shuttered windows, furniture piled everywhere. Mrs Ish. came down looking rather tired and lost, and then we went up to C's old room, only just recognizable with all the furniture gone except a piano, and the smashed windows covered. She asked me if I could say whether all the books were his: I picked one up, and it was a copy of my own novel, with that inscription in it I remember so well writing. It seemed to concentrate all our relationship, all that has gone beyond any kind of recall. We went down to the basement and planned where to put the loose books; and then talked about their family estates, and Christopher in Hollywood, all very melancholy. And then I left, and in the taxi felt tears rising uncontrollably.

Before Virginia died, I had for a long time tried to persuade her to contribute to *New Writing*. In the end she agreed to let me print the talk she had given to the Workers' Educational Association in Brighton in May 1940, which, as I have already mentioned, she called 'The Leaning Tower'. It was an extremely thoughtful talk; and particularly valuable because it rubbed in the fact that English literature had been created by the middle class; but at the same time it revealed once more the imperfection of her sympathy with the writers, poets and novelists, of a new generation – my own generation; and was surprisingly full of inconsistencies. She praised us for honest self-examination, but there seemed to be something more subjective than sober criticism when she complained that 'the bleat of the scapegoat sounds loud in their work', and that 'their state of mind as we see it reflected in their poems and plays and novels is full of discord and bitterness, full of confusion and compromise'.

I asked a working-class writer who had begun to contribute to *New Writing* before the war, the miner B. L. Coombes, Edward Upward as novelist, and Louis MacNeice as poet who had been singled out for attack, to reply in the next number of *Folios of New Writing*. I hoped that we might provoke Virginia into a further riposte, and so instigate an intriguing exchange of critical volleys; but unfortunately by the time that the spring number of *Folios* was prepared for press, Virginia was dead. I could do little more myself than write a note, as a postscript to these replies, to point out that, whatever line she may have taken in 'The Leaning Tower', she was always ready to modify her opinions – as she had written to me after the publication of the *Letter to a Young Poet* – and was, in fact, to the end, deeply interested in what young writers were struggling to express, and ready to praise any evidence of originality and imagination. B. L. Coombes wrote a calm, dignified piece, maintaining that there was in our time a tremendous urge for the working class to become articulate, and that whatever Virginia's criticism of the 'Leaning Tower' writers might be, he and his fellow-workers wanted to profit by their desire to close the cultural gap: 'I know that they can teach me much that is necessary and good. I would like to learn from them. Very probably I could tell them of things that they have never seen and they should benefit by that telling.' Edward Upward's reply was a pretty orthodox statement of a marxist position; but the most effective counter-argument, in my opinion, came from Louis MacNeice, who pointed out all the inconsistencies in Virginia's argument. The nineteenth-century writers accepted the class divisions of England? – But what about Shelley? What about the young revolutionary Wordsworth? What about William Morris? What about even Henry James who was well aware .of the trembling under the surface? Auden was a mere 'politician's poet'? – But was it not Auden who had repudiated the Public Face in the Private Place? He and his contemporaries wrote in a 'curious bastard language'? – But did not Virginia Woolf herself look forward to a future in which there would be a 'pooling' of vocabularies and dialects? And so on.

The only other thing I could do for Virginia was to see *Between the Acts* through the press at Letchworth: correct the

proofs with Leonard, choose the binding, have the jacket prepared by Vanessa, see to the Canadian edition, compose publicity
letters and design advertisements. When it came out, in the third
week of July, it was treated as a masterpiece.

From that time, the rhythm that had already established itself
before Virginia's death continued in the Hogarth Press, but with
Leonard leaving even more responsibility in my hands. We sent
one another regular reports, as we always had; I managed to get
hold of a flat in Carrington House, Hertford Street, on a longer
lease than had been possible at Athenaeum Court in Piccadilly,
and on very advantageous terms as West End flats were more or
less going begging in those middle years of the war; I made my
weekly journeys to Letchworth, and eventually persuaded
Barbara Hepworth, whose work as a land girl had not been a
success from her point of view, to come back to the Press and live
with her sister within easy walking distance of the printing
works.

At intervals, as before, I went down to see Leonard at Rodmell.
One early weekend visit, I remember, was at the beginning of
September, by which time it was clear that the tide of war had
receded from English shores, and all our thoughts and hopes were
focused on the Russian Front and North Africa. Leonard and I
talked and talked, a great deal about the war and the lessons of
history in relation to it, and about our Hogarth projects. As we
talked, I became more and more haunted by the feeling of
Virginia's presence in the house. I could hardly convince myself
that she wouldn't appear from some room at any moment, and
light one of her home-rolled cigarettes in her long holder, and
say: 'And now, John, tell us the latest scandal. . . .' On Sunday
we went over to Charleston, the first visit I had made since
Julian's death. Vanessa and Clive and Duncan Grant and Quentin
were all there. It was strange to happen on them together like
that: it increased the impression I had during the whole weekend,
of visiting ghosts, of entering a dream, particularly as Vanessa was
very silent, all too obviously still suffering under Julian's as well

as Virginia's death. She can only have been in her early sixties at the time, but she looked much older. Afterwards, at Monk's House in the evening, Leonard talked to me at length about the relationship between Clive and Virginia in the distant past, and told me the strange story of the three-cornered ménage at Ham Spray between Lytton and Ralph Partridge and Dora Carrington, which I had never heard before but is now, of course, well known. He also told me how he had discovered at least six different typescripts of Virginia's last essay on Mrs Thrale, and in addition further variants of some of the pages. We parted very happily on Monday morning, remembering I think how much we had in common, in spite of so many struggles in the past. If only it had remained so.

There was also a weekend in early November, devoted to a discussion of Virginia's literary remains. Apart from talking in a very academic way about the possibilities of peace, which neither of us really believed in, we hardly spent our time on anything else. As Leonard described to me what he had been collecting and sorting, I was absolutely staggered at the amount of essays and stories that were still waiting to be brought out in book form: work for the Press for years to come.

About a year later, we had the idea of editing between us an anthology from all the poetry the Hogarth Press had published since its foundation. The plan was to celebrate its twenty-five years of existence, and so we were going to call it *The Silver Anthology*. We even announced it in our advance lists for 1943. We decided to do the job at Rodmell, as Leonard had a complete collection of Hogarth Press publications down there, and work right through Saturday evening to Sunday afternoon. When I arrived, I found him at the back of the house, sawing wood in his old corduroys and what I had come to call his 'French poacher's' jacket. The house struck me as cold and damp, but it was filled with a great litter of books and papers and stores of the season's apples and jars of honey and jam that nevertheless created a warm atmosphere. We polished off our routine work between tea and dinner, As soon as we had eaten, we began our work on the anthology, with all the Hogarth books of poetry spread out around us.

We had not got very far when sirens sounded, followed almost immediately by a noise of gunfire on all sides and a droning of aeroplanes that seemed scarcely to stop for several hours. One or two extremely violent bursts of firing shook the house. It flashed into my mind that the Nazis could be carrying out an exceptional reprisal raid on London in answer to our raid on Berlin just before. Sure enough this proved to be so, for when I rang up the BBC at Bush House and asked to speak to my friends in the Austrian section, I was told they were all down in the shelters. The raid died down again before midnight: Leonard and I had found the situation too noisy for clear thoughts about poetry, and had returned to one of our favourite tussling arguments about the future of Germany and the organization of Europe after the war. In the middle of the night the clatter began again, with violent house-shaking gunfire and the continuous, mosquito-persistent droning of aeroplanes. We learned next morning that there had been two attacks on London, not as heavy as we could have imagined, but an opportunity on our side for a gala warning display of the terrific new London barrage that had been developed since the 1940-1 blitz. A little hollow-eyed, but nevertheless cheerful we again spent several hours crouching over the fire in the sitting room at the top of the house, picking up the little volumes, arguing but mostly agreeing, and making notes of our choices. From time to time Leonard would say: 'No, he's a hopeless poet,' or 'You know, we really *did* print rather well' (not in every case my own view), or 'That was one of Dottie's insane choices. . . .' By lunch-time we had broken the back of the job, and I left on the afternoon train for London.

I have always regretted that the gradual worsening of relations between Leonard and myself prevented *The Silver Anthology* from ever being published. It would have been a very impressive book.

Apart from editing *New Writing*, one of the most rewarding
pleasures I had in my activity at the Hogarth Press during the war
was encouraging and publishing the work of our new authors:
Henry Green, William Sansom, and the three poets: Roy Fuller,
Laurie Lee and Terence Tiller. It was one of the more curious and
unexpected results of the way the war shaped itself, that the
Auxiliary Fire Service should become a centre of literary and
artistic creation. A surprising number of writers and painters
who were not immediately threatened by the call-up volunteered
for it: among them Stephen Spender, Henry Green and William
Sansom. Henry had put his name down before the war broke out,
and of course the first year was largely occupied with the boring
routine of training, and waiting about. When the bombing began,
this subtle and complex prose artist was plunged at once into the
exhausting and violent dangers of almost nightly fire-fighting in
London. What is so remarkable is that he succeeded in keeping a
detached creator's eye alert in his inmost being throughout all his
fantastic experiences, and began to distil them in his unique
rococo prose artefacts even while the raids were in full swing. He
began in the autumn of 1940, working at intense speed in his rest
periods, completed the opening chapters of his novel *Caught*, and
then turned to several short sketches or individual episodes. He
sent me 'The Rescue' early in January and followed it with
'Mr Jonas' (which I published in the spring 1941 number of *Folios*)
very soon after. 'Mr Jonas' is as elaborately wrought as if he had
had all the peaceful leisure in the world to work at it:

What I saw, a pile of wreckage like vast blocks of slate, the slabs of
wet masonry piled high across this passage, was hidden by a fresh
cloud of steam and smoke, warm, limitless, dirty cotton wool, dis-
abling in that it tight bandaged the eyes. Each billow, and steam rolls
unevenly in air, islanding a man in a way that he can, to others, be
isolated asleep in blankets. Nor did the light of a torch do more than
make my sudden blindness visible to me in a white shine below the
waist. There was nothing for it but to go on towards voices out in
front, but climbing, slipping up, while unrolling the hose, I felt that I

was not a participant, that all this must have been imagined, until, in another instant, a puff of wind, perhaps something in the wreckage which was alight below the surface, left me out in the clear as though in, and among, the wet indigo reflecting planes of shattered tombs deep in a tumulus the men coughing ahead had just finished blasting. . . .

The idiosyncratic twists and flourishes of Henry's style seem in this passage cunningly manipulated to add to the sense of struggle and bafflement in what he is describing; and how extraordinary to be able to introduce the calm image of prehistoric tombs into this scene of nightmare. The skill with which the end of this short piece – it is only two or three thousand words long – makes its triumphant impact on the reader's mind, causes me, now that I reread it, almost to regret that Henry gradually all but abandoned such descriptive writing to pursue his theory that novels should consist almost entirely of dialogue, uncanny though his mastery showed itself in that sphere:

After twelve hours we were relieved, at half past nine in the morning. When the other crew took over we had fought our way back to exactly the same spot above that hole out of which, unassisted once he had been released, out of unreality into something temporarily worse, apparently unhurt, but now in all probability suffering from shock, had risen, to live again whoever he might be, this Mr Jonas.

I have sometimes read 'Mr Jonas' aloud to American students studying the modern English novel under my aegis. It has always left them stunned into silence.

Apparently that was not the reaction of all of Henry's friends at the time. When he sent it to me, he wrote:

I have just let a girl read it and she laughed herself into a state of tears she thought it so bad. . . . In fact she laughed so much at the first page that she put it into her mouth as you can see from the lipstick. . . . On the other hand another one three days ago liked it. Anyway I thought I'd put some commas in this time. I've tried to do it in a more spectacular way to suit the more spectacular blaze. It's true, of course, as the other one was ['The Rescue'].

In the early spring of 1943 Henry finished *Caught* and sent it to me. When I wrote him an enthusiastic letter about it, he replied:

Many thanks for your charming letter. I'm quite satisfied with *Caught* myself. I think it improves with acquaintance. The weakness is in the improbability of the story. What was intended was a series of pictures rising one out of the other, the next out of the last, with the gaps in between the silences, to mark the passage of time. But there you are. What one tries to do and what one brings off are two very different things, particularly when under the disabilities of the blitz and the difficult sort of life I make for myself.

To my surprise, and extreme annoyance, the printer started to object to certain words and phrases in the dialogue of the firemen *after* they had set up the type. The realistic quality Henry gave this dialogue wouldn't raise an eyebrow today, but in those times, with the bureaucracy only just tolerating the freedom of publishers and editors to print what they liked, Mrs Grundy could be very nasty if she wished; expecially as *Caught* could be viewed by narrow minds as a thoroughly anti-heroic book. In these circumstances I persuaded Henry to alter a number of sentences the printer's reader had marked. He was co-operative, but as indignant as I was and said he was not going to change one word more, and couldn't 'tolerate any further mucking about with *Caught*'. I wrote a strong letter to the managing director of the firm, who finally accepted Henry's alterations as the limit of the concessions we were prepared to make. It was a tricky situation, as we had all our eggs in that one basket at Letchworth. Needless to say, in such a crisis Leonard was wholeheartedly on my side. No such problems arose with that second, and totally different masterpiece, *Loving*, which we published in 1945.

Somehow or other, Henry managed to combine his service with the AFS with looking after the London office of his family engineering business. After Russia became our ally, he was involved in negotiations with the Soviet trade mission for the manufacture of various objects they were in need of; and every time I saw him he had new stories of these negotiations, so hilarious that I could scarcely get my five-shilling lunch down.

William Sansom described, in his 'Coming to London' article which appeared in the *London Magazine* many years later, how he joined the AFS when war broke out, and started to write short stories at his Hampstead station during the long bombless inactivity of the 'phoney' war; and how he was persuaded to send one of the stories to *Horizon* who promptly accepted it – to his astonishment. With this encouragement more. stories began to pour out of him, and Stephen Spender urged him to let me see some of them. I at once accepted 'Through the Quinquina Glass', and told him I was really eager to see any further stories he cared to send me. So began a very happy editor-author relationship, which lasted long after I had left the Hogarth Press and *New Writing* had come to an end. The stories in fact poured in; some of them I accepted without hesitation, others I sent back to him with letters of criticism in which I tried to explain where I thought they went wrong. He was never in a huff about this, and often rewrote them to send back to me and be accepted. Others he scrapped, or sent to other magazines, as, for one thing, *New Writing* could not cope with his bubbling creativity. The relationship was extremely stimulating to me, whatever it may have been for him: I had rarely before had to do with an author so eager to learn from his experiments, and so little disposed to bite the hand extended to him. These pleasures were crowned when I persuaded Leonard to accept the first collection of the stories, *Fireman Flower*, which we published in 1944.

Of the twelve stories in that volume only one, 'The Wall', was a straight reportage of a fire-fighting experience, though the trappings of a fireman's experiences appeared in others, as in a nightmare, to illustrate some mysterious and disturbing symbolic truth one's reason could only guess at. Sometimes he intended some more deliberate fabular construction, as with 'The Maze'; these fables did not always succeed as well as those where, as in

Kafka from whom he had obviously learnt much, interpretations could only be complex and ambiguous. Almost always one was drawn as into an intense dream, and the pleasure I found in the most successful stories came from the highly charged imaginative power he displayed, and the fact that he loved language, and was supremely, naturally interested in what could be·done with words, in recovering their latent natural force in experimental and phantasmagoric combinations. Although nothing could have been further from the dead-pan, conventionally dramatic, though highly accomplished, reportage that found so many exponents – often of much worth on a lower level – in the war years, it was nevertheless more deeply in tune with the commotion that the war stirred up in the seabed of our unconscious lives – as some of the poems that Edith Sitwell began to write at this time revealed in a different sphere.

Neither Henry Green nor Bill Sansom followed me when I broke with Leonard and founded my own publishing firm at the end of the war; their reasons were sensible and I in no way held it against them, though their presence on my list would have made a lot of difference in my struggling years. The poets, Roy Fuller and Laurie Lee, however, did, and Roy rewarded me with an excellent best-selling boys' adventure book, *Savage Gold*; while if John Lehmann Ltd. had been allowed to go on a little longer I would have had Laurie's immensely popular autobiography *Cider With Rosie*.

I have already mentioned that we published two volumes of Roy's poetry during the war, *The Middle of a War* and *A Lost Season*. In both cases some of the poems had appeared in advance in *Penguin New Writing*. He had joined up in the Royal Navy, and eventually was posted to a Fleet Air Arm monitoring unit at Kilindini in Kenya. If Bill gave me one of the most satisfying experiences in my wartime life of an editor-author relationship in connection with his stories and novels, my relationship with Roy over his poems ran it very close, though I hardly remember an occasion when I suggested the change even of a comma in those minute airgraph photo-manuscripts that reached me so regularly from East Africa, so carefully worked were the finished products and so beautifully legible his handwriting – as I had already found in the manuscripts he sent me while he was still training in England. His poems, I thought, gave the lie to those grumpy elderly panjandrums who complained so sourly in the early months of the war that there were no war poets; though Roy's work was very far in mood from that of, say, Rupert Brooke's 1914 volume, and were not at all suitable material for a Dean to recite from the pulpit of St Paul's. Apart from their extremely subtle craftsmanship and the rich precision of vocabulary, what impressed me most about them was their power of conveying the sense of the war being a profound spiritual catastrophe, as in that title poem of his first volume which begins 'My photograph already looks historic', and has as its last verse:

> The original turns away; as horrible thoughts,
> Loud fluttering aircraft slope above his head
> At dusk. The ridiculous empires break like biscuits.
> Ah, life has been abandoned by the boats –
> Only the trodden island and the dead
> Remain, and the once inestimable caskets.

Nothing more simple in expression, nothing more packed with ironic observation and deep but perfectly controlled emotion exactly suited to the times can I imagine than *Spring 1942*:

> Once as we were sitting by
> The falling sun, the thickening air,
> The chaplain came against the sky
> And quietly took a vacant chair.
>
> And under the tobacco smoke:
> 'Freedom,' he said, and 'Good' and 'Duty'.
> We stared as if a savage spoke.
> The scene took on a singular beauty.

And we made no reply to that
Obscure, remote communication,
But only stared at where the flat
Meadow dissolved in vegetation.

And thought: O sick insatiable
And constant lust; O death, our future;
O revolution in the whole
Of human use of man and nature.

The poems in *The Middle of a War* were written during his training and on his voyage by troopship to Africa. When he reached Kilindini he wrote to me:

I feel more and more that I ought to develop in some way those simple things I was writing in England. The trouble is I seem to have escaped the war again – it must be fated that there shall be no war-poets. I just have the disadvantages of noise and gregariousness without the stimulant of action. I shall have to do some nature poems – there is certainly enough nature. For the rest, discipline is sensible and the Navy, as usual, in its rather bearish, clumsy way makes us as comfortable as it can. Sixpence a day colonial money, 50 cigarettes, 2 boxes of matches and a cake of soap free every week – it is like a kind but poor and vulgar aunt. I wouldn't be in any other service for 5s. a day more! And I still find my fellow-ratings witty, kind and simple. . . .

Out of Roy's response to the natural scene around him in Kenya, the sudden fresh impact it made on him, came such beautiful poems as 'The Giraffes'. But his feeling that he ought to develop out of the 'simple things' of his first volume soon bore fruit. He began poems of more elaborate organization, expressing horror, alienation, despair, except at the memories of love, in which was mingled his vision of African tribal life, barbaric but once full of meaning, now steadily being corrupted by its absorption into an uncomprehending and uncomprehended material civilization, and his acute sense of the meaninglessness of the lives of his fellow-ratings, symbols of whose pathos and suffering he found in the animals he watched:

The monkeys near the mess (where we all eat
And dream) I saw tonight select with neat
And brittle fingers dirty scraps, and fight,
And then look pensive in the fading light,
        And after pick their feet.

They are secured by straps about their slender
Waists, and the straps to chains. Most sad and tender,
They clasp each other and look round with eyes
Like ours at what their strange captivities
        Invisibly engender.

While the battles were raging elsewhere, in his isolated station
he could reflect without sentimentality or illusion on a civilization
destroying itself by a grotesque combination of supreme technical
ingenuity and failure of moral values:

For what is terrible is the obvious
Organization of life: the oiled black gun,
And what it cost, the destruction of Europe by
Its councils; the unending justification
Of that which cannot be justified, what is done.

These two volumes of poems by Roy Fuller seem to me not
only the high point of his inspiration, but more powerful and
more original than any other poems written by serving men
during the second war, with the possible exception of Alun
Lewis's 'The Jungle' (which I first published in *New Writing and
Daylight*), Henry Reed's 'Naming of Parts', Frank Prince's
'Soldiers Bathing', and a handful of Keith Douglas's – who most
certainly would have been a poet to reckon with had he survived.

In my years of roaming round Central Europe as a poet-journalist,
I had made many friends in Bohemia and Slovakia; after the fall of
France, several of them suddenly reappeared in London and
sought me out. One I was particularly fond of and admired was
Fedor Hodža, son of the Slovak statesman, Dr Hodža, and we

began to meet for meals and drinks and long discussions on the future of the countries of Eastern Europe. One day he brought to my flat a young Czech writer by the name of Jiři Mucha, son of the famous *art nouveau* artist Alphonse Mucha. Jiři had been in France with the Free Czech forces, and the connections his family had had in the old days with France had given him the entrée to the Parisian artistic and literary world. He had innumerable stories to tell of the French writers and painters and the fate that had overtaken them when the Nazis marched in. He was also bursting with a desire to create a new cultural centre in England for his exiled fellow-countrymen and their friends among the Poles; apparently there were a number of poets, critics and dramatic experts in their midst, and he was in touch with all of them. I was carried away by his enthusiasm and seduced by his charm, and before long we were beginning to plan a new magazine together where their works could be translated and published and their problems discussed. At about the same time, while I was making my weekly visits to Cambridge from Letchworth, I came to know a brilliant young Greek poet and critic, Demetrios Capetanakis, who had come over on a British Council scholarship, and had been caught in England by the outbreak of war. He knew as much about contemporary Athenian poets and painters as Jiři knew about the Czechs, and had mastered the English language, of which he scarcely knew more than the rudiments before he arrived, in a few months. Most extraordinary of all, he had begun to write poems in English which deeply impressed me and everyone else who read them. When I told him about the plans Jiři and I were hatching, he immediately showed himself eager to organize a Greek side to the proposed magazine.

There were technical problems, of course, chief of which was the paper supply. I did not think it fair to Leonard to propose using part of the minute Hogarth paper ration for another magazine in addition to *New Writing*, but Jiři was not to be deterred. He talked to Jan Masaryk, surely the nicest and wittiest man ever to become a distinguished political figure, and managed to fire his imagination. Jiři arranged a meeting between us, and very soon after I had a telephone message from Masaryk, to say that he was going to give us all the support possible and in particular fund the paper for at least one number.

So began the publication we decided to call *Daylight*, an occasional magazine devoted to 'European Arts and Letters', with contributions by British writers as well as French, Czechs, Poles and Greeks. As it turned out, in the first volume which we brought out in the new year of 1942, the Czechs and the English predominated, though Demetrios produced translations from a major poetic work by George Seferis, a close friend of his then working in the Greek diplomatic service at Pretoria, another modern Greek poet, Pantelis Prevelakis, and an admirable and moving article of his own, 'The Greeks are Human Beings'. The call was for thinking in constructive European terms, for a future that the past offered us as a common cultural heritage, beyond the furious limits of the struggle we were all engaged in. Looking back, it seems to me that the poetry was outstanding: by Seferis, Prevelakis, Nezval, Halas, David Gascoyne, and Stephen Spender (scenes from a verse play, *Oliveiro Decides*, he never apparently finished). France could only be represented at that time by Norman Cameron's new translations from Rimbaud.

Daylight was well received, and sold well; but it soon became clear that to make it a regular publication was going to be even more difficult than we had thought. The Czechs had officially given it a generous starting impulse; but I did not want to be constantly dependent on the goodwill of one only of our European allies, or involved in inter-allied one-upmanship. Demetrios quickly understood the problem, and in our frequent discussions we finally came to the conclusion that the best, the bold thing, to do was to amalgamate *Daylight* with *New Writing* which had, after all, always been a magazine with an international slant. I was afraid that Jiři might think I was walking out on him, but when I put it to him he took it remarkably well, and soon saw that the combined magazines could have greater force and efficacy, and that the possible taint of subsidized propaganda would be eliminated from such a publication. The first number of *New Writing and Daylight* was published in the summer of 1942, and lasted for six numbers, the last, in 1946, being in fact published by my new firm of John Lehmann Ltd. The name was a bit clumsy, as names of amalgamations so often are, and gave rise to some delightfully garbled variations when orders came in from the occasional remoter bookshop: *New Writing in Moonlight* was the one I savoured most.

It was in this book-magazine that Demetrios's studies of European literary figures – Rimbaud, Dostoevsky and Stefan George – were published, between 1942 and his death from leukemia in 1944. They made a deep impression at the time, and I do not think they have ever been surpassed in their highly individual human philosophical approach.

Meanwhile my life and activities outside the Hogarth Press were changing rapidly. By the middle years of the war I was a private in the Home Guard at Bourne End, and performed my duties at weekends whenever I could; not a brilliant soldier, because on exercises I was apt to lose myself in daydreaming and find myself surrounded by the 'enemy' before I had noticed anything stirring in the shrubbery ten yards away. What I did appreciate, on guard duty by the river or up at Disraeli's Hughenden Manor, was the talk and the camaraderie of the locals, the butcher, the carpenter, the market gardener and the signalman who had in my childhood been little more than a back-drop to my protected life, and now in their nocturnal discussions revealed behind the honest smiling face of a simple village a secret scene of fiddling, black marketeering and unlicensed tobacco-growing in back gardens. When I moved into Carrington House in Mayfair I was put on the roster for fire-watching, but as by then the great raids were over, my duties consisted essentially of patrolling the roof, chatting with my fellow-watchers, and gazing at the stars.

As the war went on, and the popularity of *Penguin New Writing*, to my continual surprise, leapt from record to record, its circulation only inhibited by the paper Allen Lane was able to allocate to it, more and more letters and manuscripts poured in, sometimes hundreds in a month, and bulged from every available cupboard and drawer; most of them from the young men who had been drafted into the Army, the Navy or the Air Force, and who had been inspired by the collision of fresh and sensitive minds with extraordinary new experiences to put pencil to paper. My new secretary, Barbara Cooper, spent most of her time reading through and weeding out, skimming off those she felt most interesting and promising for me to read. She performed her task with skill, sympathy and devotion, but even so a pretty large pile had to be squeezed into my suitcase every weekend. She would pass on to me perhaps ten or twelve out of every hundred; out of these ten or twelve I would find perhaps two or three (at the most) worthy of serious discussion and a special letter. What was especially heart-warming was the occasional letter, or airgraph, which revealed how enthusiasts for *Penguin New Writing* were to be found in every part of the world the war had penetrated, and in every class. The poet Alan Ross, who became a lifelong friend after our first meeting on one of his leaves, and was at that time a sub-lieutenant in the Royal Navy, told me, to my amazement, that on board his destroyer thirty men, both officers and ratings, were eager readers of every number, passing it from hand to hand and bunk to bunk; had even reached the point of arguing about Auden on the lower deck.

In addition to these varied occupations, which, when I look back on them today, seem to me more than enough to fill an extra-energetic week, I had my one morning a week as editorial adviser to the *Geographical Magazine* (to which I had been a frequent contributor before the war) and work for the BBC and the Ministry of Information. Apart from occasional broadcasts on the current English literary scene in the overseas services of the former, I was asked to do some propaganda broadcasts on the German service, then under the top control of Graham Greene's brother Hugh, who, beneath an appearance of kindly, boyish simplicity concealed the astute mind of a trained journalist (he had come over from the foreign desk of the *Daily Telegraph*) with a shrewd grasp of political realities. These broadcasts must have met with some measure of official approval, because I was asked to start a regular series of broadcasts specifically beamed to Austria. They always started 'Lieber Pepi . . .', addressing an imaginary Austrian of my own generation whom I might have known. It was strange, rather thrilling too, to think that these broadcasts, launched into the vast of the European night, might be heard by some of my special friends of the past in enemy country. At least I was certain of one faithful listener, the monitor in Berlin – or somewhere in Austria.

My work for the Ministry of Information was all to do with Russia, and started quite unexpectedly, a few months after the Russians became our allies, with a sudden barrage of telegrams from Timofei Rokotov, editor of *Internationalnaya Literatura* in Moscow. I had got to know him during my pre-war visits to the Soviet Union, and had contributed to his magazine. Now he had decided to 'TAKE OPPORTUNITY GREET LONGSTANDING FRIEND COMRADE IN ARMS AGAINST NAZI TYRANNY'. I felt wryly amused as well as astonished by this fanfare of trumpets, as I had begun to lose my belief in the communists as natural leaders of the international struggle against fascism some time before the war when I heard the stories of volunteers returning from the Spanish imbroglio; and my change of heart had been completed by the Nazi-Soviet Pact which struck me as cynical and disgusting. My sense of confusion was clear evidence of a failure to adjust as promptly as a soldier ordered to 'About turn!' to the novel situation of the Soviet comrades being on our side. However, Rokotov, having sounded this fanfare, wanted practical co-operation on a pretty large scale: regular information about the wartime activities of British writers, regular reviews of outstanding British books as they came out, and the latest numbers of *New Writing* – if possible by air.

It was obvious to me that a door had been opened through

which some useful pro-British propaganda in the literary field
might be delivered, though I was a bit dubious about the reception
in Moscow circles of the distinctly non-rousing poetry being
written by their 'longstanding friends and comrades in arms';
but in any case how was I to cope as a simple unprivileged
civilian with all these urgent demands? Then suddenly something
unexpected happened. The new British Ambassador to the
Soviets, Sir Archibald Clark-Kerr, who had made friends with
Christopher and Wystan on their trip to China when he was
ambassador there, and had long been a keen reader of *New
Writing* according to their report, suggested in high quarters that
I ought to be used in some way to further Anglo-Russian
relations. Peter Smollett, head of the newly organized Russian
department in the Big House in Bloomsbury, telephoned me to
come and see him at once. I took Rokotov's cables along with me
to the meeting. They appeared to create a sensation. The result
was that I was encouraged, almost ordered, to send an article
each month to Moscow dealing with all the points Rokotov had
raised, with five thousand words free cabling for each article and
permission to keep for myself the fee the Russians had promised
to send.

I set to work at once, and had produced half a dozen monthly
articles when a mysterious silence fell. I was baffled, until I
received a letter from Archie: 'In case nobody has told you, I take
it upon myself to report to you the demise of "Internationalnaya
Literatura". Some say that it was euthanasia, others that it was a
painful end. It cannot have been lack of readers, for it was the
most sought after publication in the country. Nor can it really
have been lack of paper, for new publications appear. It looks
as if some of old Peter's windows on the West are being
banged.'

Soon after, the Ministry arranged for me to do much the same
kind of work for *Britanski Soyuznik*, the British newspaper the
Russians allowed us to publish over there (without any censorship
control), which had a phenomenal success. Its circulation was

severely restricted by the meagre paper ration allowed it, but copies changed hands on the black market at high prices.

One advantage of being overwhelmingly busy during the years between 1941 and 1945 was that one had no time to be worried about the fortunes of war, or seriously frightened by the V1s and V2s and the hit-and-run raids: one just had to go on working, concentrating on the task in front of one. Ten years later, I could not possibly have undertaken all that I undertook then. I can only fall back on the explanation which others have given for being able to cope with the extreme pressure of wartime duties (though many were ultimately broken by it): that danger to oneself and to everyone around one pumped some stimulating substance into one's veins, an adrenalin that tapped reserves of energy that otherwise would have lain dormant. In addition to everything else, I found time to write new poems. I noted that as soon as the distractions of peacetime returned, this vein all but dried up; it seemed to me to prove that a large part of one's time is wasted on what is worthless – or even pernicious, like salt slowly eating into silver.

Leonard, of course, was fully aware of all my activities, while he himself had his own problems, sifting through the mass of Virginia's papers, sitting on Labour Party committees, and editing the *Political Quarterly* – and sometimes giving a helping hand at the *New Statesman*. I think he realized the inevitability of it, but at the same time I also think he began to feel, understandably though in fact unjustifiably, that my attention was not always adequately focused on the Press. After all, it could not have been a full-time job, when we were producing only half as many new books as in the pre-war years.

I have come to the conclusion, when reflecting on the history of the partnership between Leonard and myself, that the unfortunate income-tax affair which blew up in 1943 did much to sour the relationship. The Inland Revenue suddenly began to query the accounts for the Press which Leonard had submitted before we became partners and before professional accountants had begun, as I and my lawyers insisted, to handle them. This was, I think, due to the fact that old stock had been selling very fast, as I have described, in the book-starved conditions of the war, and the considerable part it played in our profits could not fail to be noticed. There was nothing in the least shady about the old accounts; they were just wrong, because Leonard, with his contempt for conventional methods of doing anything, had prepared them, as he prepared his private accounts, wholly on the basis of expenditure (including printing, binding etc.) and receipts from sales. There had never been any provision in them for stock in hand at the end of a year. The result was that the Inland Revenue finally claimed a large sum in back tax from the Press. Our accountants said there was nothing to be done about it; but they did suggest that as I had had nothing to do with, and no profit from, these earlier accounts, I should claim what is technically known as 'cessation'. That meant that though I had been a full partner since 1938–9, I would not be held responsible for tax arrears before that date. My own accountants were strongly in favour of pressing such a claim, considering it only equitable; and eventually the Inland Revenue agreed. This meant that what I had to pay was very much reduced, and what Leonard had to pay similarly increased. It was a course, the accountants argued, favourable to the Press in the long run; but it was, inevitably, extremely disagreeable to Leonard at the time.

When this was settled, an extraordinary row blew up between us about Virginia's foreign rights. The crux was that Leonard kept most of the papers relating to these rights, and for that reason had in the past dealt with them (simple enough when we were all working in one house). The Press therefore made no charge if their services were called upon. Leonard suddenly asked us (in Letchworth) to look into various points connected with the rights. I pointed out that, as we had never considered these rights Hogarth Press business, and had therefore made no arrangement to charge the usual agency fee as we would with other authors, we had left most of the papers in his hands. This argument – or rather explanation – produced an explosion in which he accused me of meanness in relation to Virginia, and interference. I was horrified, and wrote to him:

I am glad you have now come into the open with your view of this episode, because it gives me an opportunity to state my view. When, at your house a few weeks ago, I saw which way you were taking it, I was so appalled that you should so wilfully misconceive me, particularly in a matter concerning Virginia, and evidently wished to start another quarrel, that I was unable to say anything and felt I had to leave the house as quickly as possible. [To the best of my recollection this was the new house he had moved into in Victoria Square, though I am not completely certain. I went on:] I never had the slightest intention of causing you any unpleasantness over this matter of Virginia's foreign rights; I initiated a careful research into it for our mutual benefit, but when you complained about the way it was being handled I pointed out that we were in some difficulty because the fact that the Press was never paid for its services in the matter had confused the question of who should hold the files of it. I did not suggest that the Press ought to be paid, though as General Manager as well as Partner I had a perfect right to suggest it; I said that we were delighted to continue to do it free, but wanted all the papers if so. I meant what I said, and I meant it politely; I would never wish to make any difficulties about V.W. and you ought to know it by now. I also meant, and continue to mean, that the Hogarth Press must nevertheless be considered as a firm, and not as the property of one or the other of us.

This row simmered down and faded out, but leaving, inevitably, a bad taste behind it. Far worse, however, in fact the worst of all our rows, was the one which preceded it – and no doubt exacerbated it. I have related how, just before Virginia's suicide, all three of us had a long discussion over lunch about Terence Tiller's first book of poems: Leonard did not altogether like it, but with Virginia and I both in favour, he yielded. In 1943 Tiller submitted a second collection, many of the poems having already been published in *Penguin New Writing*. Tiller was doing war work in Egypt, where he had become an outstanding member of the *Personal Landscape* group, which included Lawrence Durrell, Robin Fedden, Bernard Spencer and Keith Douglas. He called his new little book *The Inward Animal*.

Before I go any further, I should say that there were three books before this which I had very much wanted to publish, but which Leonard had objected to: a book of David Gascoyne's poems, which was eventually published by Poetry London with some uniquely beautiful illustrations by Graham Sutherland; a book of humorous wartime sketches, *Shaving Through the Blitz*, which had been contributed to *Penguin New Writing* by 'Fanfarlo', the pen name of George Stonier; and 'That Summer', a long short story by Frank Sargeson, in my opinion the most gifted of the younger school of New Zealand writers I had begun to publish before the war. He sent it to me at the end of 1942, and I printed it in the Penguin series in three instalments. It had an extraordinary success, and I had many enthusiastic letters about it. An English officer, in command of a unit on the Burmese frontier, sent me an airgraph after the appearance of the second instalment – the intervals between the numbers of *Penguin New Writing* had grown longer and longer – demanding to know when the third instalment was going to appear, as his men were in a state of extreme excitement and impatience to learn how the story would end. On all these three books I had deferred to Leonard's objections, though with considerable reluctance.

I was very keen to publish *The Inward Animal*, though I thought that the introduction Tiller had written for it was a mistake. Some of the poems struck me as very beautiful, and my view had been supported by the warmth of many comments when they had appeared serially in *New Writing*. Leonard, however, did not like the book at all, objecting to it on the same grounds as he had objected to the first book, but more vehemently. We both dug our heels in: I, first of all, because I admired the book, second because even if I had not liked it quite as much as I did, I would have felt it a serious mistake to drop an author whose first book had been praised for its promise and originality and who still showed those two qualities and (in my opinion) more; and third because, after the rejection of Gascoyne, I was beginning to feel, no doubt unduly subjectively, that Leonard was challenging the poetry of the younger generation as a whole, in which I had assumed he would allow me a fairly free hand.

The tussle went on from May to July. At least fourteen letters were exchanged between us during that period, some of them longer and more fulminating than any we had ever exchanged, even over the attitude Leonard had taken up over *New Writing* in 1939. Prosecuting and defending counsel poured out their denunciations of one another's cases with a stream of rhetoric worthy of a *cause celèbre*. The trouble was that this time there was no judge: Virginia was dead.

The whole business was not unlike a lovers' quarrel; in fact I have sometimes thought that our quarrels had something of the peculiar violence that erupts when two people are more emotionally involved with one another than they fully realize. Even Leonard's first letter of rejection was curiously violent. He wrote:

I return Tiller. I have read it with the greatest care and I have re-read his first book. I am afraid that I am definitely against publishing this. All the faults in the previous poems are now exaggerated and there are hardly any of their merits, except perhaps in the last poem. I do not think I am really a very stupid person, but except in the last poem the greater part of what he says is to me, except in the vaguest and most useless sense, unintelligible.... The poems are nearly always just a collection of words. I am against using our paper on this kind of thing.

More than a little shocked by the tone of this letter, I wrote back:

I am extremely sorry that you should take this intransigent attitude about *The Inward Animal*, because you must know perfectly well that I have committed myself very far in support of Tiller's promise, and in particular in support of a large number of the poems in this volume. It was your contempt of this side of the question that shocked me. If you had got me to agree to publishing a book of one of your political authors which was then a success, if that author's reputation had then steadily risen, if you had supported that rising reputation by publishing essays from his next book in the P.Q. [*Political Quarterly*], and I had then suddenly turned round with a flat veto on that book, you would feel the situation to be just as impossible as I do in this case. . . . If Tiller had been 1) a sales flop, 2) a flop with intelligent critics of poetry, there might be more to be said for asking me to desist from my encouragement of him – or if the paper involved were more than the trifle it is. It was bad enough in the case of David Gascoyne, over whose work the attitude of the Hogarth Press remains a mystery to most people I know who are interested in poetry; but this is far more serious, and raises extremely disturbing general problems of mutual trust in our relationship as partners. . . . You may possibly remember that in the case of *Amber Innocent*★ a difference of opinion (in which I stated my doubts with considerable moderation) was covered by an agreement that you and Virginia should accept responsibility for the financial loss above a certain figure.

During the next few days we had a long, inconclusive discussion in London about the whole affair, and afterwards I wrote to ask Leonard whether he would consider some compromise – presumably on the lines of the *Amber Innocent* arrangement. I reminded him that I could not remember ever having exercised a veto myself when there was a sharp difference of opinion, and went on:

In three recent cases which occurred during the war, of three authors I would have published, with varying degrees of enthusiasm, if I had been alone – Sargeson, Gascoyne, and Fanfarlo – I yielded to what I saw was your decided opposition, with varying degrees of regret, because I felt there was sufficient reason on your side for it to be against the spirit of our partnership for me to pursue my advocacy. It is, therefore, I submit, totally inaccurate to speak as if you were unable to make your views felt. The case of Tiller seems to me to be in an absolutely different class, and for the reasons I have already set out in my two earlier letters. This case, coming on top of the others, and your obvious dislike of [Henry] Green's work, which you have expressed

★ A book of poems by Joan Adenay Easdale.

with some violence in various communications to me, makes me feel
that you distrust and disbelieve in my taste and sympathies (I state this
as a fact, not as a personal matter). . . .

Henry's recently published novel, *Caught*, incidentally, had just
sold over four thousand copies, and was reprinting.

At this stage, unfortunately, the Tiller wrangle got involved in
a wrangle about the management of the Press, in which Leonard
accused me once more, with even greater acerbity than before,
of ignoring him and taking decisions without warning or consulting him and of telling him consistently that he was 'senile, out
of touch, irrelevant and petulant' – an absurd exaggeration. It
was, of course, as I realized, very difficult for someone who in the
past had supervised every detail of the workings of the Press and
every halfpenny of its expenditure, to accept that circumstances
ruled such supervision out for the time being. I wrote to him:

You very much surprised me by your new complaint that I am
ignoring you in this matter. I find it very difficult to know when you
are going to say that it is a great relief to you that I am taking petty
decisions and the routine responsibility off your shoulders, and when
you are going to say the opposite. I am constantly consulting you, but
not as much as I would like to do, for the simple reason that I cannot
spend large sums in ringing up Lewes all the time, and it is only rarely
that you let me know when you are coming to town. If you are once
more dissatisfied, you must arrange a definite time every other week,
or every week, when we can meet for business discussion. It is for you
to propose it, because I am always here.

I made one more effort to bring the temperature down about
the Tiller affair, and wrote to Leonard in June what I thought to
be a very unquarrelsome letter:

I want to ask you again whether, in view of the particular circumstances of the Tiller case, some of which may have slipped your mind
when you originally wrote, and in view of the special significance the
continued support of this author of ours had for me at this stage in his
career, which may not have been apparent to you, whether you will

reconsider your objection. I enclose some cuttings, in which you will see that some of the poems to be included in *The Inward Animal* were praised by critics who were by no means adulatory of New Writing in general. Please return them to me. I had, by the way, no intention of publishing his preface.

I enclosed cuttings from the *Times Literary Supplement*, the *Listener* and the *Observer*. But this attempt to be conciliatory only provoked another outburst of fire, a letter some nine hundred words long. In it he referred to the fact that he had agreed to reject Vita's *Grand Canyon* 'which was an extremely difficult and painful thing to do, particularly as it was the first thing submitted by her after Virginia's death'. The point, however, about *Grand Canyon* was that we *both* thought it was not up to standard; if Leonard had been really keen to publish I would certainly not have stood in the way.

The bombardment and counter-bombardment started up again, with all the wear and tear that it involved for two 'prickly people' (as Leonard described us) who were certainly feeling the strain of war conditions, even if the blitz was long over. It would be wearisome for the majority of readers to quote any further, and I have only gone into the Tiller row at some length because of its importance in portraying the difficulties of the relationship between Leonard and myself after Virginia's death, in particular the difficulties inherent in conducting a small publishing business like the Hogarth Press under circumstances that were more or less forced upon us; above all, in a sort of triangle of location.

In the end the row faded out more, I believe, owing to the exhaustion of both sides. *The Inward Animal* was published. Not long after we were amicably discussing Leonard's proposal to sell me the treadle printing press (the second), as he felt he would no longer be likely to use it himself; and the publication of Jiři Mucha's collection of short stories (some of which had first appeared in *Penguin New Writing*), *The Problems of Lieutenant Knap*, which we both liked, and Tom Hopkinson's second novel *Mist on the Tagus*.

Nevertheless the truce began to wear rather thin before the end of 1944, though we both avoided letting our differences reach the stage of increasingly acrimonious rounds of argument again. Moreover, for reasons which I intend to explain, after the war, while all my energies were devoted to making what success I could of my new publishing business, and later of the *London Magazine*, I felt that the past was the past, and sleeping dogs must be let lie. I very much admired the vitality of the autobiography Leonard began to write when he was nearly eighty, the springy step, the fresh lucidity of the prose; and said so in reviews I was asked to do of some of the volumes as they came out. In the fourth volume he spoke very fairly, and indeed very warmly of my contribution to the Press after I joined it in 1931. I was all the more astonished, therefore, to find in the posthumously published final volume, *The Journey Not the Arrival Matters* written (but not revised) more than two decades after our parting, that he had mounted an elaborate attack on me.

The point that particularly riled me, and struck me as an astonishing distortion of the facts, was his claim that during the six years (it was in fact eight years) of our partnership he 'never actually vetoed the publication of a book John wished to publish'.* The truth is that in the last phase of my association with him in the Press, our disagreements were almost entirely about books I wanted to publish and he objected to. As I have explained, before the disastrous struggle about Tiller, I had yielded over Frank Sargeson, Fanfarlo and David Gascoyne, particularly distressed to see the last-named poet go the way of Louis MacNeice and A. S. J. Tessimond (a gifted and highly individual poet who had been a contributor to *New Signatures*), though the failure of these two to be added to our poetry list was by no means so much Leonard's or Virginia's fault as Dottie Wellesley's. The failure to get Auden's poems was entirely Auden's own fault, and nobody else's. Tiller was in many ways a more important case to

* See p. 145 for his denial that a chief cause of friction had been about author-policy.

me for the reasons I have given. But coming when it did, I am
sure that part of my furious struggle not to lose him was due to
the thought at the back of my mind that the *salon des poètes
refusés* was beginning to get a little too crowded. Of my special
enthusiasms I saw only Roy Fuller and Laurie Lee remaining.

The next disagreement about an author was one of the most
painful for me. In August 1944 we were offered a first novel by
a new American author: *Dangling Man* by Saul Bellow. I was
deeply impressed by it, not because I thought it was perfect
but because I detected in it a note I had not heard struck before in
the American fiction of his generation. I sent it to Leonard with
the following letter of recommendation:

I enclose this book published by the Vanguard Press in New York
which has been offered to us, also a selection of American press
criticisms and a note from the *Manchester Guardian* which I came across
by chance. I don't think this book is a masterpiece, but there is something about it which attracts me quite a lot, and I would like to do it.
Apart from the book itself, I would like the Hogarth to be thought of
as a possible channel for the younger American writers; and the
Vanguard Press is very keen to establish fairly close relations with us.
I have just got a contract for W. Sansom's book out of them.

Leonard, however, turned down *Dangling Man*, and in so doing
lost the chance of being the British publisher of an American
writer with an exciting future, who, as everyone knows, was
eventually awarded the Nobel Prize. My enthusiasm appears to
have been a minority opinion at that time, because when, nearly
eighteen months later, I founded my own firm, I discovered that
Bellow had still not found a British publisher, and I snapped him
up at once.

Contact between the British and French intellectual worlds had
been to a certain extent re-established when the Germans and
Italians were driven out of North Africa, but it was after Paris
had been liberated in 1944 that the two-way traffic began again
with an impetuous sense on both sides of the need to make up for

lost time. The Hogarth Press and *New Writing* (which Jiři Mucha had to my delight found André Gide reading in Algiers) were evidently being talked about in literary and publishing circles on the other side of the Channel, and some wonderful opportunities came our way to pick up certain new and also certain more established French writers who had not yet found a British publisher. The most exciting of these to me was Jean-Paul Sartre, a pre-war contributor to *New Writing* and by then at the very top of public interest in France. He had become the intellectual leader of the younger generation, high priest of the new cult of atheistic existentialism, with another younger writer from North Africa, Albert Camus, as a disciple (one was told) and close competitor in influence. Camus's plays, *Le Malentendu* and *Caligula*, rivalled Sartre's *Les Mouches* and *Huis Clos* in the public fervour they aroused. But first, for me, Sartre; and I immediately put out feelers, well before VE Day. On the 12 April 1945 I was able to write to Leonard:

We have now received telegraphic confirmation from Paris that the rights in Sartre are free. Sartre, as you know, has a very high reputation in France today, and though he is not my ideal cup of tea I have always thought him most remarkable, and have published some of his stories in *New Writing*. It would, in my opinion, be excellent for the Hogarth to have him on their list. The books consist of (1) *La Nausée* (a short, rather difficult novel, or very long short story), (2) a book of short stories, of which I have already published two – in others a certain question of obscenity arises, though they are very good, (3) two excellent plays, only one of which is printed – *Les Mouches* – the other – *Huis Clos* – to follow shortly, (4) a new novel in preparation. I have already said No to the unmanageable philosophical books. What I would like to suggest is that we agree to publish, when the paper situation permits, (A) the two plays together, (B) a book containing all the printable short stories plus *La Nausée*, and that we take a first option on the novel. They are clamouring for a decision by telegraph: will you let me know what you think as soon as you can? I enclose *Les Mouches*. I think that is the one you haven't seen.

Leonard's reply, a few days later, could not have been more damping:

I return Sartre. I have grave doubts whether we should bind ourselves to publish the translations you suggest under present circumstances. Surely there will be any amount of things old and new for which we shall require paper for a long time much more worth our while than translations from the French of extremely exotic stuff which neither of us is enthusiastic about. Of course this is quite clever enough, but I am getting so tired of these retellings of the Atreidae story.

As Sartre's publishers, *La Nouvelle Revue Française*, were obviously in a great hurry for a decision, and as it would have taken several weeks to argue the whole thing out with Leonard, even if I had eventually been able to change his mind, I had to let Sartre go.

Only shortly before that Leonard had turned down Auden's selection from Tennyson, which we had also been offered. The introduction was not in my opinion one of Wystan's most acute critical writings; but I was prepared to forget my resentment at the way he had behaved over *New Year Letter*, in the hope that taking the Tennyson selection might give us the opportunity to become the publishers of all his prose work. In sending the book back to me Leonard had observed drily: 'I don't think it worth doing. His introduction is pretty thin and silly.'

I now began really to despair of my future in the Hogarth Press. What distressed me in particular about Leonard's rejections was that they seemed to show no sign of accommodation to my taste, my hunch if you like, about what was going to be significant in the emerging post-war scene. Of course, the 'generation gap' was causing a great deal of the trouble. But why then had Leonard taken in a member of the younger generation as Partner if not to do just precisely the kind of scouting he had more than once in the early days suggested he might well be losing his nose for?

The almost paradoxical fact is that in many things Leonard and I still saw eye to eye, not merely in devotion to the future of Virginia's literary remains (in spite of Leonard's almost incomprehensible outburst about her foreign rights), but also in literary and political judgements. In the spring of 1943, to a large extent I imagine owing to my work on *Britanski Soyuznik*, we had been offered a book of Soviet literary criticism, which I sent to Leonard with some observations which I have now lost. He wrote a characteristically pungent and caustically witty reply:

I return the four papers for the Soviet Literary Criticism vol. It is not an easy problem to decide. Although the papers themselves are almost uniformly fatuous, I found them personally extremely interesting. Three of the writers are almost certainly intelligent people and it is extremely interesting to see why they write such appalling rot. It is not only that all foreigners are fools, sir, what is really interesting is to see how communist, like other dogma destroys the intelligence. Another interesting thing is to observe that the intelligence in these writers is beginning to struggle against communist dogma; this is particularly obvious in the Balzac paper; a little more and poor Grib will be a heretic. The question really is whether there are a sufficient number of people who will be interested as you and I are in the objective fact of the effect of communism upon intelligence when applied to literary criticism and also whether when the four other contributions are added any one will be able to stand 60,000 words of such nonsense.

And yet even in a matter where we agreed, for instance on the impossibility of publishing the new multi-volume novel of which Stephen Spender had shown us the first part, unless it was radically rewritten, Leonard could not resist making a crack that was aimed at me as well as at Stephen: 'The trouble with Stephen and his generation is that none of them have ever grown up; they remain old undergraduates or even school boys.' This snap judgement included, one must assume, Christopher, one of the most successful new Hogarth authors, as well as Stephen and myself.

During the next few months I did some hard thinking. It

seemed to me folly not only from my own point of view, for my future as a publisher, to neglect the opportunities that were clearly opening up before me to publish new British writers who were becoming available to me through the wide success of *New Writing and Daylight* and *Penguin New Writing*, and young American and continental writers as well; but also a failure in responsibility towards those authors whose beginnings I had encouraged. In addition, *New Writing* had brought me into contact with many of the younger artists, and personalities in the world of theatre and ballet, and I saw the possibility of making the Press a centre for books on all the flourishing arts as they moved forward on the new paths they had lain down for themselves during the war. I had been deeply interested in the new flowering of the romantic visionary tradition in English painting, and had reproduced in *Penguin New Writing*, when Allen Lane allowed it, photogravure supplements, illustrations of the work of Graham Sutherland, Keith Vaughan, John Minton, Michael Ayrton and others inspired by the same ideals who had become my friends. I saw a new spirit stirring in the theatre, particularly in the production of our classics; and a vigorous indigenous school of British ballet growing up under the indomitable leadership of Ninette de Valois. All these developments were crying out, I thought, for books to study them in depth, to record, to provoke and stimulate: I wanted to provide them. It sounds a pretty heady vision; but I believed that it was real enough to pursue, and in fact much of it began to be realized when I founded my own firm after the break with Leonard. Then at last I was able to build up a lively and varied list of foreign authors, and books about the theatre, opera and ballet as well.

Leonard's terse lack of sympathy with the books I have mentioned boded ill for such dreams of development. I don't think I failed to see the advantage of having a partner who acted as a cautionary brake; it was what seemed to me the almost total refusal to let the car run at all that dismayed me. I had an unhappy feeling – admittedly only a feeling – that some more decisively negative impulse than mere caution was at work. I also feared that in the years ahead he might want to go back to what I considered were the bad habits of the old days: that system of running the Press on a shoestring, due partly to Leonard's ingrained parsimony, and partly to the way it had grown from a hobby and a small personal enterprise in the days when neither he nor Virginia were well off; a system I was sure had been responsible for the loss to the Press of several important authors, such as William Plomer and Cecil Day Lewis, and latterly Christopher Isherwood as well, with whose early works they had done so well, at least in public esteem. Never again, I vowed to myself, those damp and dusty Bloomsbury basements, those idiosyncratic methods of accounting and salesmanship, the drawbacks to which I was too inexperienced to fault in the early days when all was bathed in my eyes in the almost sacred radiance that emanated from the persons of Leonard and Virginia. For a small business, the Press was now steadily prosperous, and I was pretty sure it would not be too difficult to find the capital for expansion if more capital were needed.

At the beginning of September, before I left for my visit to liberated Paris, I decided to take what I by then believed to be the first inescapable step. I wrote a letter to Leonard explaining in as moderate and reasonable tones as I could, certainly more in sorrow than in anger, why I felt we had reached an impasse:

I was sorry you couldn't stay up for a meeting last week. It is rather too long since we had one, and I was hoping we might have been able to iron out some of our difficulties and disagreements before I went to France. As we've had no luck about the meeting, I think I had better try to put down on paper some of the things that occur to me. It seems to me that we have made rather a mess of the partnership during the last two years. Our disagreements have been various; but the most obstinate (apart from the unfortunate Income Tax business) have been about author-policy. These disagreements have appeared to me to reveal a cleavage that is unlikely to be mended in the future. I may be wrong; but if I am even partly right I fear that the partnership will be too continually near the rocks to be at all happy or tolerable in the long run.

It isn't in the least an agreeable prospect to me to dissolve the partnership, with all its association of the past and all the work I have put into it. I would much rather find some other solution. I therefore put forward the following tentative proposal. It is clear that the Hogarth could concentrate on reprints and new books by authors already accepted for some years to come, have its productive capacity full with this programme and its profits unimpaired. If we decided (without any rigidity) on this plan, would you be prepared to release me (as I would you) from the clause in our agreement preventing the partners from being associated with any other publishing venture? I don't mean I intend to join Cape, or anything like that; but possibly to found another small firm with a programme that would not be in competition with the Hogarth. You would then not have to be associated with authors who are of no interest to you; and – as long as war restrictions continue – would be able to feel that the reprinting, for instance, of Virginia's books was not being delayed for a gamble on a new author put forward by me. This would, of course, not prevent us publishing entirely new books in special cases.

I do not see that this could harm your interests (or mine); it might work to the advantage of both of us, quite apart from the harmony within the Press that it might restore.

I admit that this was a long shot; it could be considered a move of desperation; and I also admit that it showed more sanguinity about the possibility of finding additional materials (e.g. of paper) than I was later to discover was justified. In any case the gesture proved to be in vain. Leonard replied a few days later, a brief unyielding communication which I received on my return from Paris:

I have carefully considered your proposal that I should release you from the clause in our partnership agreement preventing the partners from being associated with any other publishing venture in order that you might found another small firm. I cannot agree to this as I think it would be much more likely to increase than decrease friction. If you feel that the partnership is unsatisfactory and that it should be terminated, you should take the only possible steps to terminate it. I do not agree to your statement that the chief cause of friction has been about author-policy.

My first reaction on reading this letter was a weak impulse to hide from it, to pretend it wasn't there, so great was my wish *not* to leave the Hogarth Press. However, if I was in fact more than likely to be leaving the Press (though I thought there was just a slender chance that Leonard might offer to sell out to me), I had to work out some scheme for my future as a publisher, to find sympathizers to back me, and to sound out the authors whom I had brought to the Press and see whether, if the worst came to the worst, they would follow me to a new independent publishing venture. There was also the slightly absurd situation that I could not find my copy of the Articles of Partnership which differed in some particulars from the Preliminary Scheme which I could lay my hands on. In the 'Scheme' there was no clause which prevented either Leonard or me from engaging in any other publishing business, only one which prevented Virginia from doing so once she had ceased to be a partner. Of course it was a complete fantasy to imagine that, as soon as she had my £3,000 (theoretically) in her pocket, Virginia would run off and set up as a publisher on her own, or become the shining light in, say, the family firm of Duckworth which had published her first two novels; but so we had apparently thought it necessary to lay down in those first negotiations in February 1938. Eventually, after some months, I did find the Articles, and there was no doubt that it included the clause from which Leonard refused to release me. There was also what I have called the 'blind' clause, a variation and elaboration of a similar clause in the 'Scheme'. This clause stated that if either of the partners called upon the other to dissolve the partnership, 'the partner to whom the notice is given shall have an option to be exercised within three weeks to buy out the partner giving him such notice', and if the option were not exercised within three weeks, then 'the partner giving the notice shall have a similar option to be exercised within three weeks'. I have come to think that this was far too rigid an arrangement, and in particular did not envisage any negotiations during the three weeks (on either side) which might modify what the other partner was planning or thinking. The three weeks remained quite simply a darkened room in which one partner could jump out on the other at a moment of surprise. However, I had signed it.

But there was more that needed to be settled before either of us precipitated a crisis. If there was any possibility that I might be left in sole possession of the Press, it was as much in my interest as in Leonard's that the complicated problems involved in the return of the Press to London, which included getting vacant possession from a tenant Leonard had found for the habitable rooms in No. 37 Mecklenburgh Square, and a difficult staff problem which was looming (for one thing Barbara Hepworth wanted finally to leave) should be settled first. All this took some months, and it was not till towards the end of January 1946 that I finally made up my mind to test the ice. In my letter of the 24th to Leonard I explained to him why I had not raised the matter again since our September exchanges, and went on:

I don't want you to think that I am not extremely sorry that we should have reached this point; it has been a very great disappointment to me that the harmony we finally achieved between 1940 and 1942 has been so short-lived; but equally I don't want you to be in any doubt about my conviction that the Partnership could not work in the long run after all that has happened, except with important modifications. You, however, rejected the modifications I suggested for the post-war period in my letter of 3.9.45, and you rightly drew the conclusion that the only course that was left to me was to take steps to terminate the Partnership.

I am not complaining of interference in my defined rights as Manager; I have no complaints at all there; it is a flaw more fundamental in our relationship which each successive row or disagreement has seemed to me to reveal more clearly. And if there is no more confidence between us, how can we make a success of publishing in the future? I would therefore like you to take this letter as notice in the sense of Clause 15 of our Articles of Partnership, and inform me what course you propose to follow.

I am at your disposal almost any afternoon during the coming week except Thursday to discuss procedure, which I hope we can settle without undue friction.

I was not left in the dark for long. Leonard in fact replied by return of post:

I received this morning your letter of 24 January giving me notice under Article 15 of our Deed of Partnership calling upon me to dissolve the Partnership. I shall exercise my option to buy you out on the terms provided for in that Article and this is the formal notice which I am required to give you within three weeks. It only remains to get Stocker & Mann & Co. to estimate the value of one half share in the business; will you inform them and send them a copy of the Article for their information?

In *The Journey Not the Arrival Matters* (to which I shall come back later) Leonard writes that he was 'extremely surprised' to get my letter. He goes on:

I received John's letter at breakfast, and when I had finished my kipper and coffee, I had made up my mind on what I should do about the Hogarth Press. Before lunch I had succeeded in settling its future satisfactorily. I have never been confronted more suddenly and unexpectedly by a major crisis in my affairs, and have never succeeded so quickly, completely and satisfactorily in solving it.

Leonard in this passage congratulates himself on his acumen and inspiration, but I have to say that I find it extremely difficult to understand how my letter was such a total surprise to him, and how this 'major crisis' in his affairs came upon him so 'suddenly and unexpectedly'; or how he saw me as having 'put a pistol to his head and at the heart of the Hogarth Press', as he claims later on. He may have thought my silence after his September letter indicated that he had called what he decided was my bluff, but I cannot see that that letter was anything but a direct challenge to me to go ahead and invoke the procedure laid down in the Articles of our Partnership. And in view of that, why had he not thought of any way of meeting the possibility of my taking up the challenge, before he had finished his kipper and coffee that Saturday morning?

A few days later (on the 29th) Leonard wrote to me, almost as if to somebody in his friendly confidence and not to a partner with whom he had just broken: 'I think I have arranged an extremely satisfactory method of carrying on the Press, but there has of course not been time to work out a definite detailed agreement. Everything is therefore provisional. . . .'

He describes in his book how the means to solve his crisis was 'almost on my doorstep. To be exact, it was exactly a mile and a half from Rodmell in the village of Iford, in which lived Ian and Trekkie Parsons'. Trekkie, under her maiden name of Ritchie, had produced delightful illustrations to a book for children, *The Three Rings* by Barbara Baker, which we published in 1944. She also did some paintings of Monk's House, one of which, showing the corner of the garden where stood the Donatello statue Leonard and I had bought together, I was especially attracted by and bought as a memento. Trekkie's sister was Alice Ritchie, two of whose novels the Press had published in the twenties and who had since died of cancer. While Ian was away at the wars, she and Leonard had become close friends, and Trekkie had eventually come to stay with Leonard at Monk's House. After the war she accompanied him on his visits to Israel and Ceylon. Ian was a director of Chatto & Windus, well known of course as a long-established publishing house with a very distinguished name in the literary world and, as Leonard rightly says, a back list of publications that fitted in well with the Hogarth list. Ian had, incidentally, been my contemporary at Trinity, and had always wanted to make a career in publishing (and how brilliantly he succeeded). It was with Ian that Leonard made an arrangement which provided his 'extremely satisfactory method of carrying on the Press': Chatto & Windus found the money to buy me out, and eventually Leonard became a director of Chatto while the Hogarth Press became a limited company with another director of Chatto on the board.

Looking at this development with, I sincerely think, a detachment from which all bitterness has faded, I would only like to say two things. One, that I still regret very much that the Hogarth Press, so admirable in its independence for nearly thirty years, became in effect part of a larger (though artistically first-class) business; and, two, that even under the Chatto umbrella Leonard continued to pursue a cautiously conservative policy, relying in the main on previously accepted authors – Virginia's books, the psycho-analysts, Rilke, Laurens Van Der Post, Henry Green, William Sansom, Jiři Mucha, Laurie Lee, all excellent of course (and the last-named four my own additions) – which would have left me more than a bit frustrated.

The disentangling of our partnership was long-drawn-out and difficult, and I do not think, judging from his letters to me, that Leonard at all relished the fact that he had in the end to pay me about twice what I had put into the Press; an increase which in part represented the loss in the value of money between 1938 and 1946, in part the exceptionally high sales of back stock during the war, and also in part the additional success of new authors I had brought to the Press since 1931. In their book, *A Marriage of True Minds*, Ian Parsons and George Spater observe that what I was paid for my share of the Press in 1946 made my partnership 'one of the most profitable ventures in Lehmann's long career as a publisher', but they omit to mention that it might easily have been my last venture, especially as the Paper Control refused point-blank to allow me even an ounce of paper to start up again on my own.* Leonard has said that I did not put any capital into the Press; I suppose it's a question of how you look at it, but

---

* I have had, apart from editing, only two actual publishing ventures in my life: one in the Hogarth Press, which lasted for eight years, and one on my own afterwards, which lasted for seven years.

Leonard himself did not at the time dispute the fact that at the end of 1945 the contributed capital standing in my name in the accounts was £3,500.

It has occurred to me that the reasons for Leonard's attack may have lain in what I wrote about the end of our partnership in my second volume of autobiography, *I Am My Brother*, which came out in 1960. I tried to be as fair and uncontroversial as possible, but one remark seems to have stuck in Leonard's gullet. I said that the war had turned the Hogarth Press into 'a moderately valuable property', by which I meant that it was a valuable property but (considering its size) on a moderate scale. Leonard, however, took it to imply that I thought I had by my own efforts made it at last valuable. This was a complete misapprehension.

For the next few years I was deeply preoccupied with my new publishing firm of John Lehmann Ltd, and the break with Leonard remained total. In 1952, however, I published a collection of literary essays, which I called *The Open Night*. I included in it an essay on Virginia, and asked my publisher to send a copy of the book to Leonard. He wrote back to me: 'Longmans sent me your book and I was very glad to have it. The article on Virginia is, I think, extremely good and interesting.'

It was this letter which began the rapprochement, that grew in warmth and natural ease in the course of the next ten years. Like many divorced couples, we found we had too much in common not to want to resume relations eventually. He again wrote to me in January of 1955, the year in which I published the first volume of my autobiography, *The Whispering Gallery*. I had given a radio talk on Virginia out of the material which I had prepared for the book, and Leonard had heard it. 'I rarely listen to BBC talks but I did to yours on Virginia. I thought it extremely good. What you said gave a very vivid and, I think, true picture of her. It was neither sentimental, which it might easily have been, nor artificial, but was both simple and generous.'

The following year a young man I did not know called Tom

Maschler, who was destined to make a name for himself in publishing, rang my doorbell in Egerton Crescent one morning. He had in his hand a thin, elegantly bound volume, which he told me he had found or bought somewhere and which contained what purported to be a very early piece of work by Virginia with the title of *Friendship's Gallery*. He asked me whether I wanted to acquire it. I told him Leonard must see it first. When he learned of it from me, Leonard wrote:

The typescript was offered to me for sale by Curtis Brown, from one of the Edens, as far as I can remember. It is by Virginia, but it is a kind of private joke, and not very good. I would not agree to its publication unless someone could convince me that my first impression was wrong, for I certainly did not think it worth publishing. But I was probably wrong not to buy it as I am against publishing. Would you inform whoever brought it to you that (a) I will not consent to publication, but (b) I will buy it for a reasonable price as I am against publication.

I was editing the *London Magazine* at the time, and I wrote back to Leonard: 'What I do think possible is the publication of the first two chapters, which seem to me to have a delightful and characteristically Virginian atmosphere of playful high spirits. The Japanese story [?] is a bit of a bore, but I would be very glad to publish the first chapter, or the first two chapters separately, as a fragment of Virginia's earliest known work.' Leonard, however, remained adamant in his objection to publication, and that was the last I saw of the little volume.

A month or two later Leonard wrote to me again:

I am unfortunately President of a Lewes Literary Club which has meetings on Mondays monthly in the autumn and winter. It likes to get distinguished people to address them and the Committee has asked me whether I will ask you to come and talk to us on October 22nd about some aspects of modern foreign literature, preferably French. Would you do this? It would be very nice to see you and perhaps you would come and spend the night here.

I accepted, and stayed the night at Monk's House. Afterwards I wrote in my diary: 'We fell to talking again of Virginia's methods of work. I said that I got the impression that they were constantly visiting and constantly having visitors, and was amazed that Virginia nevertheless managed to keep up such a steady and abundant output of work. Leonard thereupon said that I must remember V. and he very seldom went to a theatre or concert – it was too exciting for her; and that it was really an illusion that the social round took up so much of their time. He said that V. had worked absolutely regularly every day: from about 9.30 am to lunchtime; then took a walk in the afternoon; then after tea till dinner time worked again, or typed out what she had written in the morning, or wrote letters; after dinner there was reading or talking, but never any more work. He also told me that he had been approached to sell all Virginia's manuscripts, letters and papers in one grand deal to an American university, and thought seriously that he might do so.

In 1960 he invited me down again, to talk to his Club on the 'Problems of Autobiography', and again I accepted; again we spent a very pleasant evening together. In view of this revival of the best side of our old relationship, I was, as I have said, amazed and shocked when I read (in proof sent me by Chatto), Leonard's posthumous volume of autobiography, *The Journey Not the Arrival Matters*. In writing about the Hogarth Press, he devoted a number of pages to our relationship (and to my character) which I found all the more extraordinary as they were so sharply in contrast to the sympathetic attitude he had taken in *Downhill All the Way*.

In this volume, from which I have already quoted, he not only denied that he had ever vetoed a book I wished to publish, a mis-statement I have already dealt with, but also rebuked me, in a way which I found curiously disagreeable, for wanting to expand when the opportunity was there, and delivered a long homily on the dangers of expansion for a small publisher, which does not altogether hold water. He concluded that: 'The small "expanding" publisher has no back list of successful "bread-and-butter" books to balance his losses and overheads and is perpetually harassed by the need to raise more capital. It is not surprising that very few of these small "expanding" publishing businesses survive expansion.' But the point was that the Hogarth Press was most definitely not in that unhappy class; it had an excellent list of 'bread-and-butter' books, the chief features of which I have mentioned above. It was, I thought, totally absurd to argue that with such a back list the dangers of taking a chance on a small number of new authors every year were too great to be faced, especially when they included Sartre and Bellow. The collapse (if it can be called collapse) of my own firm John Lehmann Ltd seven years later was not due to publishing these and other brilliant international authors – American, French, Greek and Italian – who joined my list, but to other causes, the sorry tale of which I have related elsewhere – it does not belong to this story.

More pertinently, if Leonard had been alive I would have reminded him of his words in *Downhill All the Way*, about his own publishing a quarter of a century before: 'In 1920 I felt in my bones that the Hogarth Press, like the universe and so many things in it, must either expand or explode or dwindle and die; it was too young and vigorous to be able to sit still and survive.' If 1920 was the moment of truth for Leonard, 1945 was for me. And yet I cannot help thinking that there were other causes at work in changing Leonard's attitude towards our partnership, which I have never fathomed. I don't deny that I may have been unwittingly insensitive sometimes in the midst of the nerve-racking tensions of the war, and over-insistent perhaps about things that seemed especially important to me; but I always tried to keep the temperature down when I saw it was rising – and it could rise very suddenly and violently with Leonard – and tried to convince him that his interpretation of actions of mine, as in the case of the row over Virginia's foreign rights, was often quite unjustly biased. More than anything else I feel that if Virginia had still been alive events would have taken a different course; she would have mediated between us for one thing, especially when it came to differences of opinion over authors. That, of course, can only remain a conjecture.

In spite of the fact that in 1920 the Hogarth Press *did* expand, I am pretty certain myself that it could have expanded further, by gradual stages of course, if it had not been for Leonard's unalterably tight attitude towards money and also his temperamental suspicion of and incapacity to get on with the young men he brought in as managers. The opportunity came again and again, and always, as I see it, Leonard could not tolerate the idea of turning it into more than what I would call, not a Cottage but a Basement industry. He lost several authors because, having given them an excellent start under the prestige of the Press, he was unable to prevent other publishers (or agents) from luring them away by pointing (especially in the case of poets) to mean production and printing, and the primitive promotion and travelling arrangements which his parsimony prevented him from changing. The salaries he paid his employees were notoriously low, and it is a wonder (for which I have tried in part to account) that they did not resign from their work in a more rapid turnover of staff.

All that Julian had warned me about at the very beginning had come true. In spite of the charm he could switch on when he wanted, his sardonic wit and his wide knowledge of books and public affairs, especially international affairs, Leonard *had* proved overbearing, obstinate, and argumentative to a point where one felt that the desire to be argumentative became more important than the value of the argument itself. He *had* proved 'eccentric in his methods', though this eccentricity had boomeranged against himself; and he *had* attempted to be 'dictatorial' in a situation where he had signed away his right to be dictatorial. He was, it seems to me as I look back on it, caught to the last on the horns of the dilemma that emerged as soon as the Hogarth Press became bigger than a hobby: deep down he wanted his authority, his taste, to be absolute, while at the same time he knew that he had to resign part of that authority to a younger man for the Press to carry on at all. No flair in such matters as literary and artistic taste, being, as it is, to so great an extent intuitive and mysterious, is likely to last more than a certain fortunate period of years in the life of those who, to the confusion of conventional and humdrum minds, manifest it in all its revolutionary novelty. After the dazzling early years, it seems to me that the Hogarth Press, as an expression of the flair of its two founders, had all but outlived itself – except in one crucially important particular. What the Press provided for Virginia, right up to her death, was a publishing organization that allowed her to write what she liked, to experiment as her genius led her, without being checked by the doubts, the insensitivity, and the conflicting propositions of lesser minds. This, to me, is a great justification and a great honour. I have often wondered what would have happened if, in 1938, I had been able to buy the entire Hogarth Press, as it was offered to me, rather than a half partnership. I can at least say that if she had been willing to stay with the Press – and my hunch is that she would have – I would have been only too happy to allow Virginia exactly the same freedom as she had enjoyed before.

It is absurd, and deleterious, in one's later age, to harbour enduring resentments about the struggles and tribulations of one's younger career, the results of which were, after all, not entirely negative. I am still glad, and indeed much more than glad, to have had the opportunity to work with Leonard and Virginia Woolf in the Hogarth Press and to get to know them both intimately. I see myself as a neophyte, in those distant days, coming up through the olive groves to worship at the shrine of a sibyl of awesome renown, whose Pythian utterances still remain in so large a degree riddles to tease and baffle the reason, while they inspire the deepest layers of our imagination; and Leonard as the high priest, jealously guarding the frail spirit who would utter no more if his care were removed.

INDEX

Abbreviation used: L. stands for John Lehmann